# NO BULL
# ~~NOBLE~~ REVIEW™

## 500 WORLD HISTORY PRACTICE QUESTIONS

## MULTIPLE CHOICE QUESTIONS AND ANSWERS

A no-nonsense approach
for in-class review and exams

by Jeremy Klaff & Harry Klaff

## *About the Authors*

Harry Klaff taught high school social studies in the New York City public schools system for 34 years. In 1993, he was the honored recipient of the John Bunzel Memorial Award as NYC's social studies teacher of the year. As a member of city-wide Justice Resource Center, he helped write numerous curricula in law-related education. For many years, he created the annual Model City Council project, in which students took over New York's City Hall for a day-long simulation exercise.

Jeremy Klaff has been teaching AP History classes for over a decade. His website, www.mrklaff.com has been utilized by teachers and students across the country for review materials as well as original social studies music. Jeremy has been a contributor to H2 network, and has published Document Based Questions for Binghamton University's Women's History website, womhist.binghamton.edu. He has conducted staff developments for "Entertainment in Education" at both the high school and college level.

# Table of Contents

# The No Bull Approach

*No Bull Review…"because your review book shouldn't need a review book!"*

No Bull Review Books are concise and to the point. Our goal is to give you a great review for class and exams.

We, as authors of No Bull Review, are teachers. For years, we have been speaking to students to find out what you want in a review book. The answer? No Bull. You want the facts, clear and to the point. And … you want review questions. Lots of them.

This special edition of No Bull Review contains 500 multiple choice questions for World History. The practice questions in this book are our own creation, and are based on the style of questions commonly used in the curriculum. They are questions that evaluate the most important themes of World History. The goal of this book is not only to help you study for your important end-of-the-year exams, but also to provide you with a great review for the entire year. We highly recommend No Bull Review's World History Review Book to use in addition to this multiple choice edition.

We hope you enjoy the No Bull approach. Thank you, and best of luck.

— No Bull Review

# World Religions

1. Which of the following religions most resembles animism?
   A) Hinduism
   B) Buddhism
   C) Shintoism
   D) Christianity

2. Which of the following is NOT considered part of Hinduism?
   A) Karma
   B) Four Noble Truths
   C) Dharma
   D) Reincarnation

3. Aryans were
   A) Indo-European people who settled in the Indus River Valley
   B) Chinese migrants who brought Buddhism to southern areas of Asia
   C) Christian missionaries from Western Europe
   D) Jewish nomads looking to spread religion in the Middle East

4. The Mahabharata is
   A) a set of Christian dialogues from the Roman Empire
   B) a sacred text of Islam uncovered in the Middle East
   C) an epic Indian poem thousands of verses in length
   D) a Japanese scroll that reflects early religious behavior

5. Which of the following does NOT reflect the ideas of the Four Noble Truths?
   A) Parents and relationships should always be honored
   B) Selfish desires cause suffering in life
   C) People must follow a staircase of proper behavior
   D) Desires can be eliminated

6. Which of the following is NOT one of the five relationships of Confucianism?
   A) Uncle-Nephew
   B) Ruler-Subject
   C) Friend-Friend
   D) Older Brother-Younger Brother

7. Which belief system stipulates that everything has a soul and can't be harmed?
   A) Judaism
   B) Eastern Orthodoxy
   C) Sufism
   D) Jainism

8. The writings of Laozi are associated with
   A) Buddhism
   B) Confucianism
   C) Islam
   D) Daoism

9. The writings of Confucius can be found in the
   A) Mahabharata
   B) Analects
   C) Tao Te Ching
   D) Qur'an

10. Sharia law is most connected to
   A) China
   B) Argentina
   C) the Middle East
   D) Eastern Europe

11. Which of the following religions is NOT matched up with its proper writing?
   A) Judaism – Torah
   B) Islam – Qur'an
   C) Hinduism – Vedas
   D) Shintoism – Upanishads

12. Mahayana Buddhists differ from Theravada Buddhists in that they
   A) allow people to become Buddhas and permit the general population to worship
   B) interpret only the oldest teachings of Buddha
   C) discredit the ability to achieve nirvana
   D) did not spread their ideas south of modern-day China

13. In which of the following countries is Eastern Orthodoxy most prevalent today?
   A) China
   B) Greece
   C) Great Britain
   D) Germany

14. The city of Jerusalem
   A) is considered a Holy City for three monotheistic religions
   B) was populated by Muslims before Christians
   C) has always prohibited the practicing of Buddhism
   D) was settled by polytheistic followers of Abraham

15. The Diaspora refers to the
   A) proliferation of polytheistic beliefs in the Middle East
   B) spreading of Jews throughout the world
   C) split between the Pope and the Church in the Middle Ages
   D) destruction of holy Christian relics by iconoclasts

16. How did Emperor Constantine affect the spread of Christianity?
   A) He ordered all citizens in the Roman Empire to be baptized
   B) He deported all non-Christians from the Empire
   C) He ended persecutions of Christians
   D) He attacked African lands and spread Christianity to the conquered

17. Who wrote the New Testament?
   A) Moses
   B) Apostles
   C) Jesus Christ
   D) Abraham

Question 18 is based on the map below.

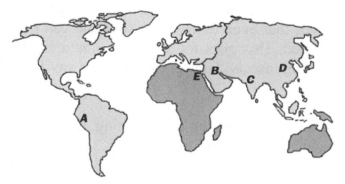

18. According to the map, what religion would one find prominent in C?
A) Islam
B) Hinduism
C) Judaism
D) Roman Catholicism

19.
• Pray five times a day
• Observe Ramadan
• Give charity to the poor

The above laws are followed by which religion?
A) Hinduism
B) Judaism
C) Islam
D) Christianity

20. The teachings of Siddhartha Gautama are most associated with
A) Buddhism
B) Christianity
C) Islam
D) Hinduism

21. A release from all suffering in Buddhism is known as
A) Dharma
B) Yin and Yang
C) Kami
D) Nirvana

Refer to the following speakers to answer questions 22-23.

**Speaker 1:** One must fast during the holy month of Ramadan when the sun is up.
**Speaker 2:** Suffering is caused by selfish desires for fleeting pleasure.
**Speaker 3:** Brahmins, Kshatriyas, Vaishyas, and Shudras each have their own class in society.
**Speaker 4:** One must accept the forces of nature, such as the balances of yin and yang.

22. Speaker 3's comment is most applicable to which religion?
A) Hinduism
B) Islam
C) Christianity
D) Shintoism

23. Which speaker is explaining a Chinese philosophy?
A) Speaker 1
B) Speaker 2
C) Speaker 3
D) Speaker 4

## Answers and Explanations

1. **C**. Shintoism, which means "the way of the gods," worships *kami*, or the spirits of nature. Shintos also practice ancestral worship. Animism is a belief that nature's animals, rocks, weather events, and plants contain spirits that affect the physical world.

2. **B**. The Four Noble Truths are part of Buddhism. The other three are associated with Hinduism. Karma means the deeds that accumulate throughout one's life. If deeds are good, then one can rise in the caste system after reincarnation (rebirth). If deeds are bad, then one's status will decrease in the next life. Dharma is a duty to honor the caste. This is done by fulfilling certain religious and societal obligations.

3. **A**. Parts of the Hindu religion were brought to India by the Aryans, or Indo-European people who settled in the Indus River Valley as early as c1500 BCE.

4. **C**. The Mahabharata is an ancient epic Indian poem detailing history. It's over 100,000 verses in length.

5. **A**. Although honoring one's parents is a good deed of behavior, it's not specific to the Four Noble Truths. Filial piety in Confucianism and The Ten Commandments of the Old Testament both emphasize honoring parents.

6. **A**. The five relationships are kept within the immediate family and public society. The two not mentioned in the choices are Husband-Wife and Father-Son.

7. **D**. Modern-day Jainism was reformed by Mahavira around 550BCE. The religion believes that everything has a soul and can't be harmed. This goes for all living creatures, including insects. Jainists cannot harm any form of life.

8. **D**. Laozi wrote the Tao Te Ching. He encouraged people to follow "the way," and accept the forces of nature, such as the balances of yin and yang.

9. **B**. Confucius wrote the Analects and advocated harmony, good conduct, and enlightenment.

10. **C**. Sharia is the religious law that governs the actions of a Muslim's daily life. Islam is prevalent in the Middle East.

11. **D**. The Upanishads are dialogues between Hindu teachers and students.

12. **A**. The Mahayana sect allows people to become Buddhas. The sect also allowed all people, not just monks, to worship. This opened up the religion to more people.

13. **B**. After a religious schism in 1054 CE, the Eastern Orthodox religion became popular in the Byzantine Empire. The religion spread to Greece and neighboring areas.

14. **A**. Jerusalem is still a holy city for the monotheistic religions of Judaism, Christianity, and Islam.

15. **B**. Jews were removed from the Roman Empire c135 CE. They then scattered throughout the world in what was known as the Diaspora.

16. **C**. Emperor Constantine had visions of a Christian cross in the heavens. He put crosses on his soldiers' shields and won an important battle. Afterward, he ended persecutions to Christians. The Edict of Milan promoted religious tolerance.

17. **B**. The New Testament of the Bible was written by disciples of Jesus known as the apostles.

18. **B**. Hinduism is most prevalent in India.

19. **C**. These are three of the five pillars of Islam. The other two are traveling to the holy city of Mecca (known as the hajj), and faith in one God, Allah.

20. **A**. Around 500 BCE, Siddhartha Gautama, a Hindu, was looking for enlightenment. He found it during a meditation session under a tree and became known as "The Enlightened One," or Buddha.

21. **D**. If one reaches the top of the moral staircase of the Eightfold Path, he or she is released from selfishness and darkness, and have achieved nirvana.

22. **A**. These are classes within the Hindu caste system. Brahmins are the priests who make up the highest class. Then come warriors (Kshatriyas), merchants (Vaishyas), and laborers (Shudras). Untouchables are those outside of the caste who are the lowest on the social ladder. A caste can't be changed during the course of one's lifetime.

23. **D**. Speaker 4 is explaining some of the philosophy regarding Daoism.

# Early Civilizations, Mesopotamia, and Egypt

1. The Neolithic Revolution was most influential in
   A) increasing the number of hunters and gatherers in Africa
   B) ending the domestication of horses
   C) establishing settled populations
   D) populating areas through nomadic hunts of wild game

2. Which geographic feature led to the thriving of civilizations in Mesopotamia?
   A) Mountains causing isolation
   B) Rivers stimulating trade
   C) Monsoons resulting in flooding rains
   D) Valuable deposits of coal

3. Ziggurats and cuneiform writing were indigenous to
   A) Indus River Valley settlers
   B) Egyptians in the Nile Delta
   C) Phoenician travelers
   D) Sumerian civilization

4. The Ganges River is most significant in tracing the roots of
   A) Buddhism
   B) Hinduism
   C) Jainism
   D) Judaism

5. Which of the following kings is paired with the empire they commanded?
   A) David – Hebrews
   B) Nebuchadnezzar II – Sumerians
   C) Hammurabi – Assyrians
   D) Hatshepsut – Babylonians

6. The maritime explorers who brought their alphabet around the Mediterranean Sea were the
   A. Hittites
   B. Phoenicians
   C. Persians
   D. Akkadians

7. Egyptian civilization was *most* affected by which geographic feature?
   A) Proximity to the Western Hemisphere
   B) Predictability of river floods
   C) Freezing winter climates
   D) Isolating mountains

8. What type of social scientist would study culture and the ways in which people lived?
   A) Economist
   B) Archaeologist
   C) Theologian
   D) Anthropologist

9. Which of the following was true of Hammurabi's Code?

A) It permitted murder and theft

B) It did not punish women

C) It was the only code of laws before 800CE

D) It did not apply to all cultures of Mesopotamia

10. King Cyrus and Asoka were similar in that both

A) displayed religious tolerance

B) increased the power of the Persian Empire

C) took over Greece

D) spread Hinduism throughout their lands

11. Along with stone, which of the following items contained the most Egyptian hieroglyphic recordings?

A) Silt

B) Papyrus

C) Mud-bricks

D) Gold

12. Nubia gained control of Egypt through which Empire?

A) Aksum

B) Kush

C) Rome

D) Phoenicia

13. Why is Mesopotamia considered to be the "cradle of civilization"?

A) It is where the earliest human fossils were found

B) The first known cave drawings were in the area

C) Early advanced settlements thrived in the region

D) It was the first place to have movable type printing

14. Mary Leakey is associated with discovering

A) the roots of the Neolithic Revolution

B) primitive farming terraces in the Andes Mountains

C) the earliest forms of ancient writing

D) the oldest known prehistoric footprints

Question 15 is based on the selection below:

"If he put out the eye of a freed man, or break the bone of a freed man, he shall pay one gold mina. If he put out the eye of a man's slave, or break the bone of a man's slave, he shall pay one-half of its value."

– Hammurabi's Code

15. Based on the above passage, which of the following was true of Hammurabi's Code?

A) Penalties were determined by a jury

B) Stricter penalties were given out to free men

C) Rights and punishments were often determined by social status

D) The kingdom abolished physical punishments for slaves

## Answers and Explanations

1. **C.** The Neolithic Revolution led to taming of animals and harvesting of crops. People could now stay in one place. Such permanent settlements led to the rise of civilizations.

2. **B.** People settled near rivers for farming, water, and trade. Mesopotamia, the cradle of civilization, was situated between the Tigris and Euphrates River in modern-day Iraq.

3. **D.** Within Sumer was the city of Ur which had pyramids called ziggurats that were used for religious worship. Cuneiform was a Sumerian system of writing which was recorded on clay tablets.

4. **B.** Typically, Hinduism's roots can be found in India near the Indus River Valley and Ganges River.

5. **A.** David was a strong Hebrew king. Nebuchadnezzar II and Hammurabi were Babylonians. Hatshepsut was one of the ancient world's few female leaders. She led in Egypt.

6. **B.** The Phoenicians were maritime explorers who also had a writing system that spread throughout the ancient world. The Latin alphabet was impacted by their writing system.

7. **B.** The Egyptians developed near the Nile Delta. Predictable Nile River floods left behind fertile soil which was necessary for civilization to emerge.

8. **D.** Anthropologists study culture and how people lived. Don't get them confused with archaeologists, who assist in excavating the artifacts needed for study.

9. **D.** Hammurabi's Code was established in Babylon of Mesopotamia, and would not apply to all civilizations everywhere in the region.

10. **A.** Cyrus of Persia allowed Jews to resettle in Jerusalem. Asoka of the Mauryan Empire favored Buddhism but was tolerant of other religions.

11. **B.** Papyrus scrolls recorded much Egyptian writing. A great deal of hieroglyphic writing was also recorded on stone.

12. **B.** Kush took control of Egypt and established a dynasty c750BCE. The Kushites lived south of Upper Egypt in a place called Nubia. Nubia gained power through trade and established an Empire.

13. **C.** The Fertile Crescent, or Mesopotamia, saw advanced civilizations thrive between the Tigris and Euphrates Rivers thousands of years ago. These early civilizations affected future societies.

14. **D.** Mary Leakey found the oldest known prehistoric footprints in Tanzania, Africa. This was a hominid, or human-like creature that could walk upright.

15. **C.** It is clear that in some cases Hammurabi's Code punished members of society differently depending on their wealth, or status.

# Early Asian and Middle Eastern Cultures

1. Put the following Chinese Dynasties in chronological order

    A. Han
    B. Ming
    C. Shang
    D. Song

A) A-B-C-D
B) D-A-B-C
C) A-C-D-B
D) C-A-D-B

2. Which river can be found in China?
A) Ganges
B) Yellow
C) Danube
D) Amazon

3. Which of the following is NOT a form of autocratic rule?
A) Dictatorship
B) Monarchy
C) Dynastic rule
D) Direct Democracy

Question 4 is based on the photo below.

4. The above structure was created to
A) establish a border between China and India
B) keep out invaders from the north
C) provide a network of aqueducts to transport water
D) prevent the erosion of farmland

5. The Qin implemented the system of legalism which encouraged
A) a strong government to keep order
B) people to follow "the way" to enlightenment
C) subjects to question all around them
D) the equality of women and men under the law

13

6. Which of the following inventions is credited to the Tang and Song Dynasties?
   A) Soap
   B) Gold coins
   C) Code of law
   D) Gunpowder

7. Which of the following was true of Zheng He?
   A) He was the first explorer to utilize the stars for navigation
   B) He traded extensively with Viking travelers
   C) His voyages occurred decades before those of Christopher Columbus
   D) He explored on behalf of the Han Dynasty

8. Women in ancient China were
   A) educated and often received high-ranking government jobs
   B) often subjected to foot binding
   C) forbidden to walk on public streets
   D) only allowed to have one child

9. Who of the following took over the most land in Asia at their peak?
   A) Mongol Empire
   B) Han Dynasty
   C) Ming Dynasty
   D) Ottoman Empire

10. Who of the following adhered to the bushido code?
   A) Chinese warrior
   B) Japanese samurai
   C) European knight
   D) Mongol horseman

11. Kabuki theater and haiku poems were cultural achievements from
   A) Japan
   B) China
   C) Korea
   D) Mongolia

12. From which Eastern Hemisphere region did the Mongols emerge?
   A) Steppe
   B) Tundra
   C) Savannah
   D) Rainforest

13. The decline of the Mongol Empire coincided with the
   A) death of Genghis Khan
   B) rise of Kublai Khan
   C) death of Kublai Khan
   D) rise of Genghis Khan

14. Angkor Wat is a complex that would have been found near which Asian Empire?
   A) Koryo
   B) Khmer
   C) Tokugawa Shogunate
   D) Qin Dynasty

15. The Deccan Plateau is an important geographical formation in
   A) India
   B) China
   C) Greece
   D) Japan

16. Which of the following was true of the Indus River Valley during ancient times?
   A) Rivers isolated India from trade
   B) The valley shielded the people from cultural interactions
   C) Complex cities emerged in the area
   D) Monotheism from the Middle East spread throughout the region

17. Which of the following Empires was found in modern-day Iran?
   A) Mauryan
   B) Gupta
   C) Mughal
   D) Safavid

18. The philosophical writings of Averroës could be found in
   A) the Middle East
   B) India
   C) Eastern Europe
   D) China

19. Which of the following Empires did NOT spread Islam?
   A) Abbasids
   B) Umayyads
   C) Moors
   D) Mauryans

20. Which of the following was true of Akbar the Great?
   A) He established a code of law for the Ottoman Empire
   B) He crossed the Great Wall of China
   C) He preached religious tolerance
   D) He constructed the Taj Mahal

21. Janissaries were
   A) elite Ottoman soldiers
   B) Mughal diplomats to Asia
   C) Abbasid princes in line for the throne
   D) religious officials in the Mughal Empire

22. All of the following were caliphs who succeeded Muhammad EXCEPT:
   A) Abu-Bakr
   B) Umar
   C) Uthman
   D) Aurangzeb

23. Which would NOT have been traded on the Silk Roads?
   A) Spices
   B) Gold
   C) Metallic objects
   D) Maize

24. The Taj Mahal was created to honor
   A) Hindu gods
   B) the wife of a Shah
   C) the sun
   D) the Ganges River

25. Ghazis were warriors who were most concerned with
   A) spreading religion
   B) securing raw materials
   C) sacrificing enemies to the sun god
   D) joining Dynastic armies in Southeast Asia

26. All of the following regions would have seen a significant spread of Islam c1400 EXCEPT:
   A) Spain
   B) Anatolia
   C) the Balkans
   D) South Africa

27. All of the following could be components of the Dynastic Cycle EXCEPT:
   A) Natural disasters
   B) Loss of the Mandate of Heaven
   C) Corruption and inner-deterioration
   D) Foundation of a new religion

# Answers and Explanations

1. **D**. Shang (c1500-1050BCE), Han (c202BCE-220CE), Song (960-1279CE), Ming (c1368-1644CE)

2. **B**. The Yangtze River in the south, and Huang He, or Yellow River, in the north, were the focal points of early Chinese civilization.

3. **D**. Autocratic rule tends to be centered within the ruler, with a lack of political participation from the subjects. Direct democracy involves political activity by the common citizen.

4. **B**. The Great Wall was constructed to keep out invaders from the northern regions of Asia.

5. **A**. Emperor Shi Huangdi (Qin Shi Huang) did not want anyone to question the Empire. Ancient writings, such as those from Confucius, were burned during the age of legalism.

6. **D**. Gunpowder was used at first for fireworks, before the Song implemented it for weaponry.

7. **C**. Zheng He traveled the Eastern World c1400 with fleets of ships much larger than those used by the Europeans a century later.

8. **B**. Foot binding was commonplace in ancient China. This was when a young girl would have each foot's toes tied to the bottom of their foot. Eventually, the foot would break, causing the young woman to shuffle. This was a symbol of male dominance.

9. **A**. The Mongols took over almost all of Asia.

They were never able to take over Japan, however, as upon their invasion, a massive storm known as a *kamikaze* destroyed their fleet of ships.

10. **B**. A samurai warrior adhered to the bushido code, or "the way of the warrior." Samurais were ready to die if that meant honoring the gods and their obligations.

11. **A**. Haikus were three lined poems about nature that traditionally had a 5-7-5 syllable scheme. Kabuki theater was a dramatic presentation that featured dance, fancy costumes, and men taking on the roles of women.

12. **A**. The Mongols were nomadic people who emerged from the Steppe (grasslands) of Eastern Europe and Asia.

13. **C**. The Empire still thrived after the death of Genghis Khan. The Empire weakened a century after Kublai's death, as famine, rebellion, overexpansion, lack of unified culture, and weak leadership broke up much of the Mongol landholdings.

14. **B**. The Khmer Empire dominated Southeast Asia c1200 in what is present-day Cambodia. Angkor Wat is an impressive temple complex in Cambodia. It was first dedicated to the Hindu god Vishnu, and later became a Buddhist structure.

15. **A**. The Deccan Plateau is a dry region that makes up most of the Indian subcontinent.

16. **C**. Around 2500 BCE, there were two cities

called Harappa and Mohenjo-Daro in the area. They had a network of roads and advanced plumbing.

17. **D**. The Safavids were Shi'a Muslims who conquered Persia (Iran). Their peak occurred under Shah Abbas.

18. **A**. The Middle East experienced a Golden Age of cultural achievement from about 750-1258. In terms of philosophy, the writings of Averroës blended religion and the philosophy of Aristotle.

19. **D**. The Mauryans were established in India centuries before the founding of Islam. The Umayyads (661-750), Abbasids (750-1258), and the Moorish Empires (711-1492) spread Islam throughout the Eastern Hemisphere.

20. **C**. Akbar the Great was known for preaching religious tolerance. Though Muslim, he gave freedoms to many Hindus. Another leader who gave religious freedom to his subjects was Suleiman the Magnificent of the Ottoman Empire.

21. **A**. Janissaries were the elite soldiers of the powerful Ottoman army.

22. **D**. Aurangzeb was an Islamic religious leader who taxed the people greatly. A caliph is a religious leader who is also the head of the government.

23. **D**. Maize was a corn product indigenous to the New World, or Western Hemisphere. The Silk Roads were trade routes that went from China, through India, and into the Middle East and Rome.

24. **B**. Shah Jahan sponsored fantastic architecture such as the Taj Mahal, which was constructed to honor his late wife, Mumtaz Mahal.

25. **A**. Ghazis were warriors who looked to spread Islam throughout the Eastern Hemisphere.

26. **D**. Islam spread through Northern Africa, and a bit further south to places such as Mali. However, it would not have a significant influence on South Africa c1400.

27. **D**. In the Dynastic Cycle: A strong dynasty came to power → They declined because of corruption and inner-deterioration → Natural disasters complicated matters and sparked revolts → This led to a dynasty's loss of the Mandate of Heaven → Then an overthrow of the dynasty → Finally, a new dynasty received the Mandate of Heaven and brought peace. Then, the cycle repeated itself.

# Greece, Rome, and the Byzantine Empire

1. A polis that functioned as an oligarchy
   A) acted as a socialist government
   B) was controlled by a powerful and wealthy elite
   C) tended to be a representative democracy
   D) was ruled solely by a monarch

2. The author of the *Iliad* was
   A) Virgil
   B) Homer
   C) Confucius
   D) Averroës

3. Direct democracy refers to a government where
   A) many of the local citizens can govern the affairs of a polis
   B) representatives are elected to govern the people
   C) the citizens share the factors of production
   D) censorship eliminates opposition to the state

4. Which of the following was NOT an element of classical Greek architecture?
   A) Doric, Ionic, and Corinthian columns
   B) A symmetrical layout
   C) Stone construction
   D) Pointed arches

5. *"The unexamined life is not worth living."*
   The above quote can be attributed to
   A) Socrates
   B) Plato
   C) Alexander the Great
   D) Aristotle

6. In *The Republic*, Plato argued that
   A) government should be controlled by the intelligent
   B) the planets of the solar system revolve around the sun
   C) rule based on heredity was necessary for stability
   D) the scientific method was needed for experimentation

7. Hellenistic culture refers to the
   A) blending of cultures throughout Alexander the Great's Empire
   B) ideas exchanged on the Silk Roads
   C) spread of culture throughout the Roman Empire
   D) developments that occurred during Pax Romana

8. Plebeians were
   A) aristocratic Romans
   B) dictators within the Roman Republic
   C) opponents of the Twelve Tables of Law
   D) commoners of Rome

9. Which of the following is true of the rivalry between Athens and Sparta?
A) Sparta had developed a greater sense of cultural achievement
B) Sparta defeated Athens in the Peloponnesian War
C) Athens defeated Sparta at Troy
D) Both Athens and Sparta were defeated in the Persian Wars

10. Which geographic feature isolated Greek city-states from one another?
A) A lack of harbors
B) Volcanic activity
C) A mountains mainland
D) Deserts in northern Greece

Question 11 is based on the photo below.

11. The above structure is known as the
A) Pantheon
B) Roman Forum
C) Parthenon
D) Temple of Zeus

12. The Punic Wars were a battle between
A) Athens and Sparta for control of the Greek mainland
B) Greece and Rome over trading rights in the Aegean Sea
C) Rome and Carthage for power in the Mediterranean region
D) Rome and Anatolia over the spread of religion

13. Which leader was famous for marching his troops, horses, and elephants through the French Alps during the Punic Wars?
A) Hannibal
B) Scipio
C) Caesar
D) Cato

14. Julius Caesar
A) refused to give citizenship to any conquered territories
B) opposed land reform for the poor
C) conquered land in Greece, Western Europe, Egypt and Asia Minor
D) adopted Christianity into the Roman Empire

15. Which of the following exhibits culture from Western Civilization?
A) The writings of Confucius
B) Euclid's *Elements*
C) The Temple of Kukulkan
D) Great walls of Zimbabwe

16. Many of the cultural advances of Rome took place
A) during the years of Pax Romana
B) within the age of Caesar
C) before Augustus took power
D) just before Rome fell in 476CE

17. Aqueducts in the Roman Empire were used for
A) centers of entertainment
B) transporting water
C) storing weapons
D) training warriors

18. Which of the following empires preserved the most Roman culture?
    A) Ottoman
    B) Mughal
    C) Byzantine
    D) Khmer

19. Justinian's Code
    A) legislated against heresy
    B) decreased the rights of slaves
    C) provided for separation of Church and state
    D) was based on Hammurabi's Code

20. Which of the following had the greatest influence on the religious schism between East and West c1054?
    A) Two officials claimed to be Pope
    B) There was warfare between two capital cities
    C) The use of icons was questioned by the West
    D) The selling of indulgences was condemned by the Church

21. What region made great use of Cyrillic writing?
    A) Russia
    B) Italy
    C) Anatolia
    D) Mesopotamia

22. To which city did Vladimir the Great and Yaroslav the Wise bring Christianity?
    A) Moscow
    B) Yalta
    C) Saint Petersburg
    D) Kiev

23. Raids by both Germanic tribes and Attila the Hun precipitated the fall of
    A) Rome
    B) Greece
    C) Constantinople
    D) Alexandria

Questions 24-25 are based on the selection below.

"**Table IX.**
    "4. The penalty shall be capital for a judge or arbiter legally appointed who has been found guilty of receiving a bribe for giving a decision.
    "5. Treason: he who shall have roused up a public enemy or handed over a citizen to a public enemy must suffer capital punishment.
    "6. Putting to death of any man, whosoever he might be unconvicted is forbidden."

"**Table X.**
    "1. None is to bury or burn a corpse in the city."

24. The above laws are attributed to which city?
    A) Athens
    B) Sparta
    C) Rome
    D) Byzantium

25. Which is true according to the above laws?
    A) capital punishment is illegal
    B) betraying the state and judicial system is a fate worthy of death
    C) trials were not used to determine guilt
    D) in times of peace a merciful justice system prevailed

## Answers and Expanations

1. **B.** An oligarchy is ruled by a powerful and wealthy elite.

2. **B.** Homer wrote the *Iliad* and the *Odyssey*. The *Iliad* was set during the Trojan War. This is the story where the Greeks hid inside a wooden horse to sneak into Troy.

3. **A.** Athens, whose leader was Pericles c450BCE, supported a direct democracy where the local male citizens would govern. It should be noted that women and slaves had no political power.

4. **D.** Pointed arches came much later, and are associated with Gothic architecture during the Middle Ages.

5. **A.** Socrates believed in questioning the world around him. The government found him guilty of corrupting the youth of Athens. He was sentenced to death.

6. **A.** In the Republic, Plato indicated that an efficient government must be controlled by the most intelligent leaders, or philosopher-kings.

7. **A.** Alexander the Great's Empire spanned much of the Eastern Hemisphere. He helped to blend Greek, Persian, Egyptian, and Indian cultures into a cultural diffusion example known as Hellenistic culture.

8. **D.** Plebeians were commoners, which included merchants and farmers. For many years, they could not hold high office. They eventually received a voice in the Senate, becoming elected officials called tribunes.

9. **B.** In 431 BCE, Sparta declared war on the Athenians. Because of Sparta's military advantage, Athens surrendered in 404 BCE. The war devastated the Athenian government and led many to question the efficiency of democracy.

10. **C.** Mainland Greece is mountainous, which made it difficult to link ancient city-states. This led to isolation. However, since Greece is surrounded by water on three sides, it made the peninsula perfect for sea-travel.

11. **C.** The Parthenon in Athens is probably the world's most famous example of classical architecture.

12. **C.** Competing for trade in the Mediterranean, Rome fought the Punic Wars with Carthage of northern Africa. There were three wars fought between 254-146 BCE.

13. **A.** In the Second Punic War, Carthage's Hannibal looked to attack Rome from the north. He never captured it, as a Roman general named Scipio defeated him near Carthage.

14. **C.** At the peak of his power, Caesar was a dictator and controlled land all over the Eastern Hemisphere. Christianity was yet to be founded at the time.

15. **B.** Western Civilization refers to the Greco-Roman culture which laid the foundation for life in Europe. Science, mathematics (Euclid made discoveries in geometry), and literature were just some of these cultural achievements.

16. **A.** Pax Romana was a time of about 200 years of peace from 27 BCE to 180CE. It coincided with the rise of Augustus, and led to vast trade and cultural advances.

17. **B**. Aqueducts were stone and concrete structures, typically on arches, that distributed water to the population.

18. **C**. The Byzantine Empire was the Eastern Roman Empire. It preserved Roman culture in modern-day Eastern Europe and beyond.

19. **A**. Justinian's Code provided laws against heresy, or clashing with the established religion. It also gave more rights to slaves and expanded marriage rights for women.

20. **C**. The split occurred partly because of the use of icons, or images used in prayer. From Rome, Emperor Leo III declared icons to be synonymous with idol worship. As the religious practices of Eastern and Western Europe drifted apart, there was an eventual split where the Eastern faction became Eastern Orthodox, while the Western one continued to practice Roman Catholicism.

21. **A**. When Russia became independent from Mongol rule in 1480, influences of Byzantine culture were still present. One example is the Cyrillic alphabet, which has connections to Slavic people who traded in Constantinople.

22. **D**. Vladimir the Great and Yaroslav the Wise brought Christian ideas to Eastern Europe, notably in Kiev.

23. **A**. Rome fell in 476CE. It collapsed because of economic issues including inflation and failing agriculture, and political factors such as overexpansion.

24. **C**. These are excerpts from the collection of laws known as the Twelve Tables of Rome.

25. **B**. In the excerpt, one can see that capital punishment (death) is a penalty for treason, and for judges taking bribes.

# Africa, Native America, and the Age of Exploration

1. Which area of Africa has been suffering the greatest degree of desertification?
   A) Steppe
   B) Rain forest
   C) Mediterranean
   D) Sahel

2. Bantu people, as early as 2000BCE, were responsible for
   A) spreading language throughout Africa
   B) trading enslaved people to Europe
   C) living exclusively in nuclear families
   D) denying the validity of a patrilineal society

3. The most important trade network in Western Africa c1000CE was the
   A) triangular trade
   B) gold-salt trade
   C) silk trade
   D) diamond trade

4. Mansa Musa impacted Mali mostly by
   A) abandoning the trading of salt
   B) introducing Islam to his people
   C) being the first African leader to sell subjects into slavery
   D) adopting the economic system of manorialism

5. Swahili combines elements of Bantu and
   A) Latin
   B) Greek
   C) Russian
   D) Arabic

6. Ibn Battuta was known for his
   A) discoveries in astronomy
   B) travels throughout the Eastern Hemisphere
   C) philosophical writings
   D) help in spreading religion throughout the Middle East

Questions 7-8 are based on the map below.

7. Which Empire would be found in A?
   A) Mayan Empire
   B) Incan Empire
   C) Aztec Empire
   D) Mughal Empire

8. Which civilization can be found near E?
   A) Mali
   B) Songhai
   C) Egypt
   D) Zimbabwe

9. Which of the following Native American Empires flourished most recently?
  A) Zapotec
  B) Nazca
  C) Moche
  D) Aztec

10. What type of building structures were set up by the Anasazi?
  A) Clay-bricked pueblos
  B) Symmetrical stone dwellings
  C) Wooden single-family homes
  D) Two-story symmetrical granite structures

11. Which Native American civilization would be considered Mesoamerican?
  A) Inca
  B) Chavín
  C) Maya
  D) Nazca

12. Which is true of the Mayan Empire?
  A) They had a system of writing
  B) Despite building cities, they did not construct pyramids
  C) They eliminated Spanish threats to their land
  D) They lacked a religious story of creation

13. Terrace farming was used by agricultural workers as a means to
  A) produce crops during drought
  B) harvest plants from deep within the soil
  C) establish farms in the mountains
  D) replenish the soil with fertilizer after harvest

14. Caravels and astrolabes were important inventions that led to achievements in
  A) factory construction
  B) algebra
  C) exploration
  D) harnessing of hydroelectric power

15. All of the following were motivations of European explorers c1500 EXCEPT:
  A) A quest to gain great wealth
  B) A belief that cultures should be converted to Christianity
  C) A hope to bring glory to the countries of sponsorship
  D) A desire to populate far off lands with European offspring

16. The Line of Demarcation and the Treaty of Tordesillas allowed Portugal to become strong in which modern-day country?
  A) Peru
  B) Brazil
  C) Venezuela
  D) Panama

17. Which explorer found a direct sea route to India for spices and other trade?
  A) Christopher Columbus
  B) Vasco da Gama
  C) Ferdinand Magellan
  D) Francisco Pizarro

18. Why was Hernando Cortés most likely able to conquer the Aztecs?
  A) The use of advanced weapons
  B) Treaties with foreign nations
  C) Offering generous land grants
  D) Providing new trade markets in Spain for the natives

19. The *encomienda* system was used by the Spanish as a means for
  A) trading spices and cloth
  B) migrating populations to the Pacific Ocean
  C) removing resources through forced labor
  D) providing rights to the native population

20. Which of the following was true of the Columbian Exchange?
A) Europe received horses from the New World
B) There was a decrease in slavery in the Americas
C) Diseases spread throughout the New World
D) Corn was introduced in the New World

21. Which of the following terms is most associated with the slave trade?
A) Middle Passage
B) Peninsulares
C) Mercantilism
D) Commercial Revolution

22. Which of the following statements was true of mercantilism?
A) It looked to extract raw materials from the Mother Country
B) It expanded the power of the colony
C) England was the only country to take part in mercantilism
D) Finished products were made in Europe

23. The Commercial Revolution refers to a time period when
A) slavery decreased in the New World
B) *encomienda* reached its peak
C) Europeans turned to socialism
D) international trade increased

24. In the Spanish colonies, Mestizos were
A) those born of African and European ancestry
B) people who held high office in the New World
C) inhabitants of European and Native American ancestry
D) Spaniards living in the New World who were born in Spain

25. Who of the following had the greatest power in the New World?
A) Creoles
B) Peninsulares
C) Mestizos
D) Mulattos

## Answers and Explanations

1. **D**. The Sahara Desert has been expanding southward to a region called the Sahel. When grassy regions dry up, it's called desertification.

2. **A**. Tribal languages had similarities because they derived from the migrations of the Bantu people. Many of today's African languages date back to these ancient travelers.

3. **B**. Ghana grew rich because of the trade of gold. Much gold was traded for salt.

4. **B**. Mansa Musa converted to Islam, went on the hajj, and brought the religion to Mali.

5. **D**. In Eastern Africa, because of contact with Middle Eastern countries, a new language called Swahili emerged. It combined African Bantu and Arabic.

6. **B**. Ibn Battuta was a North African traveler who ventured for 29 years throughout the African and Muslim world. He also went as far as Asia, and Eastern and Western Europe. His observations are of interest to those comparing the strengths of world empires, and cultural diversity in the mid-fourteenth century.

7. **B**. The Incas lived in the Andes Mountains near modern-day Peru.

8. **C**. It's important to note that Egypt is in Africa, just not in Sub-Saharan Africa (below the Sahara Desert). Zimbabwe is further to the southeast. Mali and Songhai would be in western Africa.

9. **D**. The Aztecs were still strong when Europeans encountered them in the Age of Exploration. The other empires peaked centuries earlier.

10. **A**. The Anasazi lived in the modern-day American Southwest. They constructed pueblos, or cities made from adobe (clay-bricked) architecture.

11. **C**. The Mayans lived in Mesoamerica near modern-day Mexico and Central America. The other civilizations were further south.

12. **A**. The Mayan Empire peaked from about 250-900 CE. They set up complex cities in Tikal in Guatemala, and Chichen Itza in the Yucatán. The Mayans had an understanding of math, astronomy, and a written language that was composed of glyphs, or symbols. Their most celebrated work was the Popol Vuh, their story of creation.

13. **C**. Terraces were like steps that went up a mountain. This allowed farming to be done on the slopes of the Andes. In addition, when it rained, water and nutrients would be washed down the steps, as opposed to running off.

14. **C**. The Portuguese built caravels, or small fast-moving boats with large sails. An astrolabe (or mariner's astrolabe) was used to locate stars, the moon, and planets to aid in navigation.

15. **D**. Although it would happen over the centuries, the c1500 motivations for the explorers can be summed up in three letters: GGG. Gold, God, and Glory.

16. **B**. Spain and Portugal were the two early powers of exploration, and they fought over land in the New World. In 1493, Pope Alexander VI attempted to bring peace. He drew a *line of demarcation* on a map and said that Spain would get everything west of it, and Portugal would get the land to the east. In 1494, the Treaty of Tordesillas moved the line a bit to the west to give Portugal more territory in modern-day Brazil. Today, this is why most people in South America speak Spanish, yet Brazil to the east speaks Portuguese.

17. **B**. Vasco da Gama found a direct sea route to India. Columbus discovered the New World, Magellan circumnavigated the Earth, and Pizarro conquered the Incas.

18. **A**. Cortés conquered the Aztec Empire and Montezuma II in 1521. Though outnumbered, use of advanced weapons and gunpowder, as well as the recruitment of the Aztec's enemies, led the Spanish to victory.

19. **C**. Victories for the Spanish in the New World led to a massive collection of gold and other riches. The Spanish forced Native Americans to help remove such resources in a labor system called *encomienda*. Though it was supposed to be fair, *encomienda* resembled slavery, as rights were denied to the natives. By 1550, Spain ended this practice.

20. **C**. One of the greatest examples of cultural diffusion, the Columbian Exchange was the trading of all plants, animals, and resources between Europe and the Americas. A consequence of this trade was the spread of disease, of which Native Americans were not immune.

21. **A**. The Middle Passage was the Triangular Trade's central journey which brought slaves from Africa to the Caribbean. As for the Triangular Trade, molasses from the Caribbean was brought to New England, distilled into rum, and then traded to African kings for the slaves.

22. **D**. Mercantilism is an economic system where the European Mother Country (whether it be Spain, France, Netherlands, or England) extracted raw materials, such as gold or tobacco, from the colonies. They sold homemade finished goods to the colonies as well. The sole purpose of the colonies was to make the Mother Country rich and self-sufficient.

23. **D**. The expansion of international trade and colonization led to new business ventures. This time of opportunity was called the Commercial Revolution and lasted from the late fifteenth century until the seventeenth century.

24. **C**. Mestizos are those in the New World who were of both European and Native American ancestry.

25. **B**. In the New World, from most powerful to least, you should know: Peninsulares, or people born in Spain who could hold the highest offices in the New World, and Creoles, or Spanish people who were born in the New World. Along with the Peninsulares, they controlled most of the wealth. In addition, mestizos were people of European and Native American ancestry, mulattos were people of African and European ancestry. Finally, there were Native Americans, the most numerous, with the fewest rights.

# The Middle Ages

1. Which event did NOT take place during the Middle Ages (500-1500)?
   A) Hundred Years' War
   B) Invention of the printing press
   C) Crowning of Charlemagne
   D) Punic Wars

2. Who of the following had the greatest power in the hierarchy of feudalism?
   A) Knights
   B) Lords
   C) Vassals
   D) Serfs

3. Pepin the Short and Charlemagne were associated with the
   A) Carolingian Dynasty
   B) Byzantine Empire
   C) Vikings
   D) Magyars

4. Feudalism was strong in Europe before 1500 because
   A) there was a shortage of farmable land
   B) threats from invaders fostered a need for military service
   C) an absence of capital made fiefs a commodity
   D) most peasants were given the opportunity to train and become knights

5. Troubadours were known for their
   A) strategic use of longbows
   B) work in the field of alchemy
   C) spreading of Christianity to Asia
   D) performing of music in castles

6. Guilds were influential in
   A) distributing philosophy throughout the fragmented plains of Europe
   B) protecting the working rights of artisans
   C) trading with the people of Western Africa
   D) protesting the Roman Catholic Church's sale of indulgences

7. The Hanseatic League looked to
   A) protect trading rights such as freedom of the seas
   B) monopolize trade in Asia
   C) isolate territories on the Baltic Sea
   D) compete with the trading of salt on the Silk Roads

8. Lay investiture occurred when
   A) people were kicked out of the Church
   B) Church members were denied salvation
   C) kings appointed rich nobles to religious offices
   D) sacraments were sold to those not worthy

9. Compared to Gothic churches, Romanesque churches

  A) contained stained glass windows

  B) included flying buttresses which linked walls

  C) could only be found in Eastern Europe

  D) were symmetrical with rounded arches

10. John Wycliffe was targeted by the Church because he

  A) sold sacraments without the Pope's approval

  B) attacked the power of the Pope

  C) was accused of simony

  D) hammered the 95 Theses to a Church door in Germany

11. Which of the following was a lasting result of the Crusades?

  A) The Christians were able to take over the Holy Land

  B) An exchange of goods and ideas took place across regions

  C) Northern Africa became Christian

  D) Islam dominated Northern Europe

12. Which statement is true of the Crusades?

  A) Richard the Lionheart reached an agreement that allowed Christians to enter the Holy Land

  B) Pope Urban called for the Third Crusade

  C) Saladin was the Muslim commander during the First Crusade

  D) The Crusaders were Protestant armored knights

13. The goal of the Spanish Inquisition was to

  A) terrorize those who challenged the power of the Moors

  B) deport all traitors against Islam

  C) eliminate opposition to Roman Catholicism

  D) control the weights and measures of grain

14. In the *Summa Theologica*, Thomas Aquinas wrote

  A) using both Christian theology and Greek philosophical thought

  B) about the abuses of the Catholic Church

  C) a dissenting opinion concerning fighting in the Holy Land

  D) persuasive articles which led to a reformation of the Church

15. In the Great Schism of 1378-1417

  A) Eastern Orthodox emerged in Eastern Europe

  B) two popes claimed to be legitimate

  C) the Eastern and Western Roman Empires separated

  D) new religious sects were created in England

16. Which of the following was a result of the Black Death?

  A) Decreased prestige for the Catholic Church

  B) Increased trading between Europe and Asia

  C) A more stable feudal system

  D) The end of the Hundred Years' War

17. Joan of Arc was instrumental in aiding
    A) the French during the ascendancy of William the Conqueror
    B) Crusaders during the Third Crusade
    C) the French during the Hundred Years' War
    D) the English during the Battle of Hastings

18. Which of the following led to greater European harvests during the Middle Ages?
    A) Extensive terrace farming
    B) The Three-Field System
    C) Slash-and-burn farming
    D) Mechanical farming techniques

Questions 19-20 are based on the selection below.

"In the first place we have granted to God, and by this our present charter confirmed for us and our heirs forever that the English Church shall be free, and shall have her rights entire, and her liberties inviolate; and we will that it be thus observed; which is apparent from this that the freedom of elections, which is reckoned most important …

"We have also granted to all freemen of our kingdom, for us and our heirs forever, all the underwritten liberties, to be had and held by them and their heirs, of us and our heirs forever."
    – Runnymede, England, 1215

19. The purpose of the above charter was to
    A) reform the Catholic Church
    B) limit the power of the King
    C) ensure favorable trading rights on the Mediterranean
    D) produce a line of succession to the throne

20. What long-term effect resulted from the above charter?
    A) A decrease in freedom of speech rights
    B) Greater influence of the representatives in Parliament
    C) The escalation of absolutism in England
    D) A direct democracy in England

## Answers and Explanations

1. **D**. The Hundred Years' War (1337-1453), Gutenberg's Printing Press (c1440), and the crowning of Charlemagne (800) all took place during the Middle Ages. The Punic Wars took place during the time of ancient Rome.

2. **B**. Below is a simple hierarchy of the feudal system in Europe.

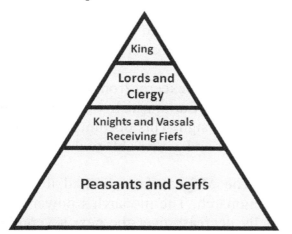

3. **A**. When Pepin the Short took the title of "King by the Grace of God," the Carolingian Dynasty began. Pepin's son was Charlemagne. Under Charlemagne's reign from 768-814, his Carolingian Empire controlled more land than the Byzantines.

4. **B**. The Middle Ages were a harsh time where invaders (Vikings, Magyars, and Muslims) looked to plunder European lands. Feudalism was a political and economic system that involved land ownership and military service.

5. **D**. Troubadours sang about the themes of love and honor. They were key performers in an age of chivalry. Chivalry was a code of conduct where a knight fought honorably for the lord and his lady.

6. **B**. Guilds, similar to today's unions, protected the working rights of artisans of a similar craft. The guild members were *masters* of their trade. Before becoming a master, one had to be an *apprentice* for another master, and then a wage-earning *journeyman*.

7. **A**. In Northern Europe near the Baltic Sea there was a commercial organization known as the Hanseatic League. States in modern-day Germany, Sweden, Poland, Latvia, Estonia, and more, formed this organization to protect trading rights such as freedom of the seas, and fair weights and measures. It was strong from the thirteenth through seventeenth centuries.

8. **C**. Lay investiture occurred when kings and rich nobles appointed religious officials. This would give them an unfair influence over the Church. Though the Church was powerful, activities such as lay investiture were viewed by many as corrupt.

9. **D**. Romanesque churches were symmetrical with rounded arches and towers. Gothic churches were ornate with pointed arches, stained-glass windows, and flying buttresses that linked walls.

10. **B**. Around 1380, Wycliffe said that Jesus Christ was the true head of the Church, not the Pope. In addition, around 1400, Jan Hus preached that the Bible was of a higher authority than the Pope. Hus was excommunicated and burned at the stake.

11. **B**. Though violent and creating much religious strife, the Crusades created new trade networks between Europe, Asia, and Northern Africa. Not only were goods and innovations exchanged, but scientific and mathematical thought as well.

12. **A**. King and Crusader Richard the Lion-heart was able to secure the right of Christians to visit the Holy Land in 1192. Pope Urban called for the First Crusade in 1095. Saladin fought in the Third Crusade. The knights were Roman Catholic. Protestant sects emerged years later.

13. **C**. In the Inquisition, a tribunal interrogated those seen as heretics (people with beliefs that clashed with the Catholic Church). Typically the oppressed were Jews, Muslims, or recent converts to Christianity.

14. **A**. Aquinas was a religious scholar who wrote the *Summa Theologica* c1274. His work is a combination of Christian theology (study of religious faith) and Greek philosophical thought, specifically from Aristotle. Aquinas' followers were called *scholastics*.

15. **B**. Unlike the schism of 1054 which divided religion between Eastern Orthodox and Roman Catholicism, this schism was *within* the Catholic Church. Two people declared themselves Pope; Pope Urban VI in Rome, and Clement VII of Avignon, France. Eventually, a different Pope was elected.

16. **A**. The bubonic plague ultimately hurt the prestige of the Church as prayers went unanswered. The plague further weakened the stability of the feudal system as well.

17. **C**. The Hundred Years' War wasn't really 100 years. But from 1337-1453 England and France were engaged in battle. In the war, a French girl named Joan of Arc saw visions from God and felt compelled to save France. Although Joan led the army to victory, she was later captured and accused of heresy and witchcraft. She was burned at the stake in 1431.

18. **B**. In the Three-Field System, land would be farmed into sections. One of those sections would be left unfarmed so the soil could rejuvenate. This led to greater harvests.

19. **B**. This is an excerpt from the Great Charter, or Magna Carta which was forced upon King John to sign. This document limited the king's power and gave rights to the people.

20. **B**. The Magna Carta limited the power of the monarch. The monarch's power would gradually decrease over the next several centuries. This resulted in the increased power of Parliament.

# The Renaissance and Protestant Reformation

1. What country is considered to be the birthplace of the Renaissance?
   A) Italy
   B) France
   C) England
   D) Spain

2. What was humanism?
   A) A religious doctrine that expressed good deeds to mankind
   B) The takeover of one culture by another
   C) A cultural and philosophical movement
   D) The belief that there was no meaning of life

For questions 3-7, identify the correct Renaissance artist.

    A. Hans Holbein
    B. Jan van Eyck
    C. Leonardo da Vinci
    D. Michelangelo
    E. Raphael

3. Painted the *Mona Lisa*

4. Sculpted the *Pietà*

5. Painted the *School of Athens*

6. Painted *The Last Supper*

7. Flemish realist painter

8. Which of the following was a result of Johann Gutenberg's printing press?
   A) An increase in the use of Latin
   B) The writing of books in vernacular
   C) An abandonment of movable type technology
   D) The spreading of the newly written words of the Magna Carta

9. Niccolò Machiavelli advocated for which type of ruler?
   A) One who was ruthless and could maintain power
   B) A monarch who was enlightened and ready to share the state's wealth
   C) A dictator who gave many freedoms to the people
   D) One that provided democracy to all subjects

10. What has become the greatest contribution of the Elizabethan Age?
    A) Colorful oil paintings
    B) Shakespearean literature
    C) A written constitution
    D) Musical symphonies

11. All of the following have been considered causes for the Protestant Reformation EXCEPT:

A) The selling of indulgences

B) Resentment of the Pope's power

C) A desire for monarchs to centralize their power

D) A belief that the Bible was more important than the power of the clergy

12. In the 95 Theses, Martin Luther specifically

A) questioned the authority of the Bible

B) stated that bishops could give salvation

C) criticized the selling of indulgences

D) showed that faith was inconsequential for getting into heaven

13. In the Peace of Augsburg

A) the religion of German states was left up to local rulers

B) Catholicism was outlawed in all German states

C) Protestantism was outlawed in all German states

D) peasants voted for the first time to establish a religion

14. John Calvin impacted religious thought by

A) establishing that the Pope's power was absolute

B) providing a new interpretation of the Bible

C) preaching that God has planned the fate of all people

D) expressing that salvation exists for everyone

15. In the year 1610, which country would have been mainly Roman Catholic?

A) England

B) Hungary

C) Russia

D) Spain

16. What was the Counter-Reformation (Catholic Reformation)?

A) A backlash within the Catholic Church to reform itself

B) A movement by monarchs to secure power from the clergy

C) A measure to continue the sale of unwarranted indulgences

D) A procedure to create more Protestant sects

17. Which of the following was a result of the Protestant Reformation?

A) Division between religious sects

B) Increased power of the Catholic Church

C) A decrease in the amount of Presbyterians

D) The dominance of the Anglican Church in Rome

Questions 18-19 are based on the selection below.

"Albeit, the King's Majesty justly and rightfully is and oweth to be the supreme head of the Church of England, and so is recognised by the clergy of this realm in their Convocations; yet nevertheless for corroboration and confirmation thereof, and for increase of virtue in Christ's religion within this realm of England, and to repress and extirp all errors, heresies and other enormities and abuses heretofore used in the same, Be it enacted by authority of this present Parliament that the King our sovereign lord, his heirs and successors kings of this realm, shall be taken, accepted and reputed the only supreme head in earth of the Church of England..."

– Act of Supremacy, 1534

18. The above Act resulted in
    A) the spread of Roman Catholicism to England
    B) an increase in power for Henry VIII
    C) the end of Anglicanism in England
    D) an increase in power for the Pope

19. A major factor that helped lead to the above legislation was
    A) the condemnation of simony
    B) a desire for England to acquire papal land in Rome
    C) the King's desire to divorce his wife
    D) a hope to weaken French religious authority in the region

# Answers and Explanations

1. **A**. Italy borders the Mediterranean, and is a perfect port for economic commerce and trade. In addition, Italy's social roots were based on the classical traditions of Greco-Roman culture. The Italian Renaissance was centered in Florence where the influential Medici family ruled the city by 1434.

2. **C**. Humanism was a cultural and philosophical movement that celebrated a person's achievements. Whereas the Middle Ages stressed studying Christianity, humanism looked to investigate the classical teachings of ancient Greece and Rome. Humanists expanded education in subjects called humanities (social studies, literature, philosophy, languages). They wanted to *secularize* society, or make it worldly instead of religious.

3. **C**. Leonardo da Vinci was truly a "Renaissance Man," as his talents went beyond art. Among other things he was an inventor, scientist, sculptor, and writer. His best known painting is the *Mona Lisa*.

4. **D**. Michelangelo sculpted the *Pietà* which portrays the Virgin Mary holding her son, Jesus, after the crucifixion. His statue of the *David* was completed in 1504 and today can be found in Florence. The statue is both a symbol of strength and a celebration of the human body. Michelangelo also painted the ceiling of the Sistine Chapel in Vatican City.

5. **E**. Raphael painted *Madonna and Child*. He also painted the *School of Athens*, which is a c1510 masterpiece where Plato walks with Aristotle. It is a *fresco*, which is a work of art painted on damp plaster, typically on walls.

6. **C**. Leonardo da Vinci also painted *The Last Supper*.

7. **B**. North of Italy, Flemish painter Jan van Eyck was successful using oil paints. Hans Holbein was a German artist.

8. **B**. Literature became more widely available because of Johann Gutenberg's invention of the printing press. The Gutenberg Bible was one of the earliest works printed in Europe. Because of this new use of movable type, learning spread throughout Europe at a much faster pace. Further increasing education, many writers abandoned Latin and wrote books in *vernaculars*, or local/native tongues. The Magna Carta was in 1215, well before the printing press was invented (c1440).

9. **A**. Niccolò Machiavelli wrote *The Prince* in 1513. In this work he explained that a strong leader must rule harshly to keep order. Otherwise, people would walk all over that leader. Therefore, a ruthless personality is needed to not only secure power, but hold onto it.

10. **B**. The Elizabethan Age refers to the Renaissance period in England that coincided with the reign of Queen Elizabeth I from 1558-1603. Elizabeth Tudor was a patron of the arts who sponsored artistic endeavors. During this time, William Shakespeare of England wrote and produced comedies such as *The Merchant of Venice*, and tragedies like *Hamlet* and *Macbeth*. Note: The Renaissance experienced in England, France, and Germany is known as the *Northern Renaissance*.

11. **C.** The Reformation stemmed from those who contested the selling of indulgences, (or paying off sin without being punished), resentment to the Pope's power, and a belief that the Bible was more important than the power of church officials. Although King Henry VIII would centralize more power during his reign, it was not a direct cause of the Reformation.

12. **C.** Martin Luther contested the selling of indulgences. Luther believed that the Bible was the authority of Christianity, not the clergy. He also believed that only God could give salvation to heaven. In addition, to get into heaven, one must have faith in God's forgiveness.

13. **A.** In the 1555 Peace of Augsburg, the princes agreed to allow the ruler of each German state to determine if it would be Catholic or Protestant.

14. **C.** Influenced by the teachings of John Calvin, Calvinists preach *predestination*, or the concept that God has planned the fate of all people. This means that only certain souls can find salvation. Calvinist principles spread to France, Netherlands, and Switzerland. It was also adopted by Presbyterians in Scotland.

15. **D.** Modern-day Spain, France, Italy, and Ireland were mostly Catholic, while modern-day England, Germany, and Scandinavia were predominately Protestant. Russia and Greece were Eastern Orthodox.

16. **A.** The Counter-Reformation was an attempt by the Catholic Church to reform itself and keep church members from leaving. Beginning in 1545 at the Council of Trent, Catholics condemned selling unwarranted indulgences and reaffirmed the importance of the Bible. They also stated that good works, as well as faith, were necessary for salvation.

17. **A.** The major outcome was division between religious sects. Furthermore, the Roman Catholic Church, which had been so powerful during the Middle Ages/Age of Faith, was negatively impacted.

18. **B.** In 1534, Parliament (the legislature of England) passed the Act of Supremacy. This made Henry the head of the Church of England, and thereby increased his authority.

19. **C.** The Church did not allow Henry to annul, or declare his marriage invalid. He decided to break away from the Church. Because he was now independent of Rome, Henry could divorce his wife Catherine.

# Absolutism and Enlightenment

1. Which concept best reflects the belief that European monarchs were representatives of God on Earth?
   A) Divine right
   B) Mandate of Heaven
   C) Theocracy
   D) Filial Piety

Use the following monarchs to answer questions 2-5.

    A. Charles I
    B. Frederick the Great
    C. Ivan the Terrible
    D. Louis XIV
    E. Philip II

2. He secured Silesia from Maria Theresa in 1748.

3. He defended Catholicism in Spain.

4. He restricted the powers of the boyar nobles.

5. He was executed during a domestic conflict.

6. The legislating against the rights of Huguenots was greatest in
   A) France under Cardinal Richelieu
   B) Austria under Maria Theresa
   C) England under Henry VIII
   D) Russia under Peter the Great

7. One legacy left behind by Louis XIV for France was
   A) heavy debt brought about by expanding the Palace of Versailles
   B) decreasing the gap between the rich and the poor
   C) state support for Enlightenment philosophy
   D) eliminating religious turmoil

8. The significance of the Spanish Armada's defeat was the
   A) elimination of Spain in the New World
   B) dominance of England in North America
   C) overthrow of Philip II
   D) decreased power of the European nobility

9. The primary cause of the Thirty Years' War was
   A) religious differences
   B) commercial investments abroad
   C) turmoil in overseas colonies
   D) succession to the Austrian throne

10. The Peace of Westphalia resulted in
   A) the end of Protestantism in Central Europe
   B) the end of the Bourbon reign
   C) a decrease in Hapsburg power
   D) the Defenestration of Prague

11. Which war between Britain and France resulted in the greatest loss of French colonies in the New World?
    A) War of Spanish Succession
    B) Seven Years' War
    C) Thirty Years' War
    D) War of Austrian Succession

12. All of the following were examples of Peter the Great's westernization of Russia EXCEPT:
    A) A building of a new capital city
    B) Expanding education
    C) Encouraging the growing of beards
    D) A move to a new calendar

13. Which Stuart King, and cousin of Elizabeth Tudor, was known for a new translation of the Holy Bible?
    A) James I
    B) James II
    C) Charles I
    D) Charles II

14. Cavaliers were concerned with
    A) supporting the King
    B) expanding natural rights
    C) favoring Catholicism
    D) limiting the power of the aristocracy

15. All of the following were outcomes of the English Civil War EXCEPT:
    A) the execution of Charles I
    B) the issuance of the Bill of Rights
    C) a military dictatorship under Oliver Cromwell
    D) extension of Puritan rights

16. The Restoration refers to the resumption of the monarchy under which Stuart?
    A) James II
    B) William of Orange
    C) Charles II
    D) Oliver Cromwell

17. The 1688 Glorious Revolution was notable for being
    A) bloodless
    B) the last revolution in Europe for two centuries
    C) the final overthrow of the monarchy
    D) a global conflict

18. The guarantee of the accused to go in front of a judge before a sentencing is called
    A) *writ of mandamus*
    B) *habeas corpus*
    C) Magna Carta
    D) *stare decisis*

19. What happened to the power of the English monarchy from 1215-1689?
    A) The monarch became a figurehead
    B) A constitutional monarchy was established
    C) Parliament lost its power
    D) Vast amounts of land had been lost

For questions 20-22, link the following four scientific thinkers to their achievements.

A. Nicolaus Copernicus    B. Galileo Galilei
C. Isaac Newton    D. Andreas Vesalius

20. Illustrated the heliocentric model

21. Proved that objects of different weights fall at the same speed

22. Established laws of universal gravitation

23. Philosophers such as Francis Bacon and René Descartes
    A) confirmed the truth behind Aristotle's observations
    B) were instrumental in bringing an end to the age of absolutism
    C) used math and reason to prove their theories
    D) spread religion from England to the Balkans

24. Enlightenment philosophers looked mainly to
    A) expand liberties and natural rights
    B) disprove religious law
    C) affirm the notion of divine right
    D) spread learning to the poor

25. *"I disapprove of what you say, but I will defend to the death your right to say it."*
The above quote can be attributed to
    A) John Locke
    B) Jean-Jacques Rousseau
    C) Baron de Montesquieu
    D) Voltaire

26. • The Legislative Branch creates the laws.
    • The Executive Branch enforces the laws.
    • The Judicial Branch interprets the laws.

The above ideas were illustrated most succinctly by
    A) Baron de Montesquieu
    B) Denis Diderot
    C) Mary Wollstonecraft
    D) Claude Monet

27. Which of the following quotes is attributed to Jean-Jacques Rousseau?
    A) "…that all men are created equal, that they are endowed by their Creator with certain unalienable rights"
    B) "Absolute power corrupts absolutely"
    C) "…hath by nature a power, not only to preserve his property, that is, his life, liberty and estate"
    D) "Man is born free, and everywhere he is in chains"

Question 28 is based on the photo below.

28. Which type of architecture is in the above picture?
    A) Baroque
    B) Realism
    C) Impressionism
    D) Classical

29. Enlightened despots were most likely to support
    A) an end to fighting wars
    B) figurehead rule
    C) the arts and education
    D) revolutions in Europe

30. Which of the following artists was NOT considered an impressionist or post-impressionist artist?
    A) Vincent van Gogh
    B) Edgar Degas
    C) Claude Monet
    D) Denis Diderot

Questions 31-32 are based on the selection below.

"Man being born, as has been proved, with a title to perfect freedom, and an uncontrouled enjoyment of all the rights and privileges of the law of nature, equally with any other man, or number of men in the world, hath by nature a power, not only to preserve his property, that is, his life, liberty and estate, against the injuries and attempts of other men; but to judge of, and punish the breaches of that law in others, as he is persuaded the offence deserves, even with death itself, in crimes where the heinousness of the fact, in his opinion, requires it."
    – John Locke, *Second Treatise of Government*

31. In the above selection, John Locke specifically advocates
    A) the protection of free speech rights
    B) freedoms from unreasonable search and seizure
    C) protection of possessions
    D) abolishment of capital punishment

32. Which of the following would John Locke most likely support?
    A) Habeas Corpus Act
    B) Edict of Nantes
    C) Edict of Milan
    D) Act of Supremacy

## Answers and Explanations

1. **A.** Many monarchs (kings and queens) ruled with complete power from c1500-c1740. As seen in ancient China (Mandate of Heaven) and Egypt (theocracy), there was a belief that the king was the representative of God. In Europe, this theory was called *divine right*.

2. **B.** Frederick the Great was from modern-day Germany and fought the Hapsburg queen Maria Theresa in the middle of the eighteenth century.

3. **E.** Philip defended Catholicism as Protestantism spread throughout Western Europe. Though becoming rich under Philip, Spain ultimately squandered its mercantilist fortune and went into economic decline.

4. **C.** Ivan the Terrible was a czar (Russian king) who restricted the powers of the Russian nobles called boyars.

5. **A.** Charles I was sentenced to death during the Puritan Revolution (English Civil War).

6. **A.** Because Louis XIII was a weak king, Richelieu became his powerful official. Richelieu favored Catholicism in France, and legislated against French Protestants called Huguenots. Huguenots had been given freedoms previously with the 1598 Edict of Nantes.

7. **A.** Nicknamed "The Sun King," Louis said *"I am the state."* He expanded the Palace of Versailles into one of the most elaborate compounds in the world. Complete with thousands of rooms, ornate statues, and extensive gardens, this symbol of France was built at the expense of the suffering and starving peasants. Louis XIV fought many wars during his 72-year reign. Although France became a strong force, weaker countries teamed up against them to keep French territorial gains minimal.

8. **B.** In 1588, Philip's Spanish Armada was defeated by England. In time, the English became the supreme naval force in the world.

9. **A.** This war began with the Defenestration of Prague when Protestants threw three Catholics out of a window (they survived). Thus, the war was caused by religion.

10. **C.** In the Peace of Westphalia that ended the Thirty Years' War, the Hapsburgs lost power in the region, and France gained some land.

11. **B.** Known as the French and Indian War in North America (which began in 1754), the Seven Years' War saw Britain defeat France to maintain their colonial Empire in the New World and India.

12. **C.** Beards were seen as a Mongol influence. Peter the Great looked to emulate Western Europe and modernize Russia.

13. **A.** After Elizabeth Tudor (Elizabeth I) died with no heir, the Stuart family ruled England. James I, a cousin of Elizabeth's, assumed the throne. During his reign came a new interpretation of the Bible (King James Bible).

14. **A.** Cavaliers were supporters of King Charles I of England. They were defeated in the English Civil War.

15. **B.** The Bill of Rights came later, in 1689. Charles I and his supporters were defeated by General Oliver Cromwell in the Puritan Revolution/English Civil War (1642-1649). Charles was brought to trial by the Puritan victors, and was executed for treason. Cromwell ruled as a military dictator until 1658.

16. **C.** With the people longing for a return of the monarchy, Charles II resumed Stuart rule in 1660.

17. **A.** Aided by her Dutch prince husband William, Mary overthrew James II in a bloodless revolution in 1688.

18. **B.** During the reign of Charles II, the *Habeas Corpus Act* was passed by Parliament. It guaranteed the accused a right to go before a judge. One could not just be thrown into prison.

19. **B.** As centuries progressed, a limited, or constitutional, monarchy prevailed with Parliament having immense strength in the creation of laws. The monarch still had power, but was not absolute.

20. **A.** The heliocentric model was Nicolaus Copernicus' belief that the planets revolved around the sun. This idea contrasted with the geocentric model that declared the Earth to be the center of the universe.

21. **B.** Galilei was a scientist who discovered that objects of different weights fall at the same speed (this went against Aristotle's theory). He also observed the moons of Jupiter and confirmed Copernicus' theories.

22. **C.** Newton researched universal gravitation and created three laws of motion. Vesalius, the choice not used, gave new ideas on anatomy and how to perform surgery.

23. **C.** Philosophers such as Francis Bacon and René Descartes attacked the scientific conclusions made by Aristotle. Descartes relied on math and reason to prove his theories. This use of observation developed into the Scientific Method. The Scientific Method was a new sequence of investigation that was used to test a hypothesis through experimentation. After logical steps were taken, a conclusion could be derived.

24. **A.** Enlightenment philosophers used reason to define the liberties which they thought people should have in nature.

25. **D.** In the eighteenth century, Voltaire wrote hundreds of essays regarding the themes of freedom of speech, religion, and other social reforms. He was a supporter of separation of church and state.

26. **A.** Montesquieu illustrated the concept of separation of powers, where the Legislative Branch (makes laws), Executive Branch (enforces laws) and Judicial Branch (interprets laws) controlled the government. All three would operate under a system of checks and balances that would prevent one branch from getting too strong. Separation of powers was adopted by numerous nations, including the United States.

27. **D.** Rousseau said that government should rule for the common good. A famous quote of his was that, "Man is born free, and everywhere he is in chains." Here, Rousseau was describing unjust laws which prevent natural rights and liberty.

28. **A.** In the Age of Absolutism, many castles displayed baroque architecture, which was usually colorful, ornate, and rather lavish.

29. **C.** A despot is another term for an absolute ruler. Enlightened despots were those who supported the Age of Reason. Rulers such as Frederick the Great of Prussia and Catherine the Great of Russia supported modernization. They embraced the arts, education, religious toleration, and an end to certain torture punishments.

30. **D.** Denis Diderot was an editor for the *Encyclopédie* in France which printed many essays. The essays supported Enlightenment ideas and looked to change the way people viewed government. In the nineteenth century, French artists such as Edouard Manet, Edgar Degas, and Claude Monet froze their impressions of a moment in time. This art movement is called *impressionism*. Some artists, such as Dutch painter Vincent van Gogh, concentrated more on emotions. These artists are known as post-impressionists.

31. **C.** This selection from Locke advocates for the preservation of property, liberty, and one's estate.

32. **A.** Of the choices, Locke would most likely support the right to go before a judge, as stipulated by the Habeas Corpus Act.

# The French Revolution, Napoleon, and Latin American Independence

1. Which of the following was consistent with the Old Regime of France?
   A) A Second Estate made up of the clergy
   B) An oligarchy that governs without the consent of nobles
   C) A king whose power is greatly limited by Parliament
   D) A Third Estate made up mostly of peasants

2. Why were members of the Third Estate most dissatisfied with the Old Regime of France?
   A) They were not allowed to vote
   B) They paid disproportionately high taxes
   C) They could not move freely within the country
   D) They were denied access to farming equipment

3. Which Revolution inspired the other three?
   A) American Revolution
   B) French Revolution
   C) Haitian Revolution
   D) Venezuelan Revolution

4. Louis XVI and Marie Antoinette were viewed by much of the bourgeoisie as
   A) efficient leaders who helped France grow stronger
   B) enlightened despots
   C) British sympathizers
   D) unfit to meet the needs of the people

5. Put the following events of the French Revolution into chronological order:

   A. Storming of the Bastille
   B. Execution of Robespierre
   C. Legislative Assembly declares war on Austria
   D. King Louis XVI is put on trial

   A) A-B-C-D
   B) C-A-D-C
   C) A-C-D-B
   D) C-B-D-A

6. The oath taken by the National Assembly at a tennis court promised
   A) a new constitution for France
   B) intervention in the American Revolution
   C) ratification of a peace treaty with Austria
   D) an end to the Reign of Terror

7. The primary purpose of the Committee of Public Safety was to
   A) make sure that France was secure from foreign attack
   B) spy on the King and Queen of France
   C) spread the words of the Enlightenment
   D) decide who were traitors and enemies of the Republic

8. All of the following were members of the Jacobins EXCEPT:
   A) Maximilien Robespierre
   B) Paul Marat
   C) Georges Danton
   D) Olympe de Gouges

9. The Great Fear occurred when
   A) King Louis XVI dismissed the Estates General
   B) rumors of violence spread throughout France
   C) Napoleon came to power in Paris
   D) Robespierre targeted traitors with the guillotine

10. The Bastille would best be described as a
    A) castle
    B) prison
    C) marketplace
    D) noble's mansion

11. The French Directory was
    A) a moderate five-member executive
    B) influential in removing Napoleon Bonaparte from power
    C) responsible for writing the *Declaration of the Rights of Man*
    D) a radical faction within the Jacobin party

12. In the Battle of Trafalgar, Napoleon
    A) gained control of the English Channel off the coast of Britain
    B) lost nearly his entire army and was banished to Elba
    C) suffered a crippling naval defeat
    D) succeeded in enforcing his Continental System

13. Which of the following was true of Napoleon's Code?
    A) It gave equal rights to all men and women
    B) Freedom of speech was limited
    C) French factories were divided up amongst the peasants
    D) Direct democracy was enforced

14. Which of the following led to Napoleon's first banishment?
    A) Continental System
    B) Peninsular War
    C) Battle of Waterloo
    D) Invasion of Russia

15. During the Hundred Days, Napoleon did all of the following EXCEPT:
    A) Escape Elba
    B) Gather supporters in the countryside
    C) Lose at Waterloo
    D) Defeat the British on their soil

16. Which of the following is consistent with the beliefs of Klemens von Metternich?
    A) Restoration of legitimate monarchies
    B) Shifting the balance of power to Eastern Europe
    C) Supporting revolutions
    D) Outlawing alliances

17. The Concert of Europe was
    A) an alliance looking to protect against uprisings
    B) a philosophical fraternity of Enlightenment thinkers
    C) an organization for the spreading of democracy
    D) an economic union linking Europe to Latin America

Use the following leaders to answer questions 18-19.

    A. Simón Bolívar
    B. José María Morelos
    C. José San Martin
    D. Toussaint L'Ouverture

18. Was known as the *Liberator* of Venezuela

19. Helped lead a slave revolt in Haiti

20. Which Mexican politician favored the liberal movement La Reforma?
    A) Benito Juárez
    B) Miguel Hidalgo
    C) Agustín de Iturbide
    D) Antonio Lopez de Santa Anna

21. Which of the following countries gained its independence from Portugal?
    A) Argentina
    B) Haiti
    C) Brazil
    D) Peru

22. Which of the following had the greatest impact on Latin American revolutions during the nineteenth century?
    A) The end of the *encomienda* system
    B) The Enlightenment and French Revolution
    C) The Treaty of Tordesillas
    D) The end of the Commercial Revolution

Questions 23-24 are based on the selection below:

"The representatives of the French people, organized as a National Assembly, believing that the ignorance, neglect, or contempt of the rights of man are the sole cause of public calamities and of the corruption of governments, have determined to set forth in a solemn declaration the natural, unalienable, and sacred rights of man…
"Articles:
"1. Men are born and remain free and equal in rights. Social distinctions may be founded only upon the general good.
"2. The aim of all political association is the preservation of the natural and imprescriptible rights of man. These rights are liberty, property, security, and resistance to oppression."

23. The above excerpt was taken from the
    A) Congress of Vienna
    B) *Declaration of the Rights of Man and of the Citizen*
    C) Napoleonic Code
    D) Declaration of Independence

24. Which Enlightenment thinker was widely known for the ideas expressed in Article 2?
    A) Voltaire
    B) Denis Diderot
    C) Baron de Montesquieu
    D) John Locke

## Answers and Explanations

1. **D**. The Old Regime was the historic class and political structure of France under the monarchy. It included the First Estate, the clergy, who owned a great deal of land. Then came the Second Estate, or nobles, who also controlled a great amount of wealth. Finally, there was the Third Estate, which was divided into the bourgeoisie (well-educated artisans and capitalists) and the peasants. Peasants made up most of this Estate.

2. **B**. The Third Estate made up about 98% of the people. Despite not having most of the wealth in France, they paid more than their fair share in taxes. They also had little say in government.

3. **A**. The success of the American Revolution, along with the Enlightenment ideas that inspired it, helped bring about other revolutions around the globe.

4. **D**. The King and Queen were seen as out of touch, and inefficient leaders. While people starved in France, they spent money on a lavish lifestyle. They also spent a great deal of money supporting the Americans against the British in the American Revolution.

5. **C**. Storming of the Bastille (7/14/1789), Legislative Assembly declares war on Austria (1792), King Louis XVI is put on trial (1793), Execution of Robespierre (1794).

6. **A**. Locked out of an Estates General meeting, National Assembly (Third Estate) members broke into an indoor tennis court. There, they took an oath to make a new constitution for France.

7. **D**. Robespierre seized power. He wanted to rid France of people who supported nobility and the monarchy. To do this, he established the Committee of Public Safety to sniff out enemies of the Republic.

8. **D**. Olympe de Gouges spoke out for female equality. She was unsuccessful in her campaign, and was executed during the Reign of Terror. The Jacobins were a revolutionary political club that wanted to eliminate all aspects of monarchy and make France a Republic. The Jacobins turned to violence to achieve their goals. Their leaders were Paul Marat, Georges Danton, and Maximilien Robespierre.

9. **B**. In the aftermath of the Bastille violence, there were riots and mob chaos. Fueled by rumors that both the King and the first two Estates were going to imprison or kill peasants, hysteria unfolded known as the Great Fear. Peasants armed themselves with whatever they could and paraded through the streets. Many looted the homes of nobles.

10. **B**. A symbol of absolutism in France, the Bastille was a prison that housed political prisoners. Although King Louis XVI began to listen to the demands of the people, he also called in neutral (Swiss) troops to protect France from mob rule. Nonetheless a crowd overtook the Bastille. This event triggered the first bloodshed of the Revolution, which today is celebrated in France as Bastille Day.

11. **A**. In the aftermath of the Reign of Terror, a moderate five-member executive branch known as the Directory took over alongside a two-house legislature. The Directory appointed Napoleon Bonaparte to lead France's army.

12. **C**. Trafalgar was a naval battle that Napoleon lost to British commander Horatio Nelson off the coast of Spain.

13. **B**. To legislate for his Empire, a legal code was named in Napoleon's honor. Although the code gave equal rights to all men under the law, it limited freedom of speech. Furthermore, women's rights were decreased and male dominance was protected.

14. **D**. When Napoleon got deep enough into Russia, Czar Alexander I ordered the land to be burned (called scorched-earth policy). This destruction of agriculture left Napoleon's army to starve through the harsh Russian winter. He lost almost his entire force of half a million soldiers during the campaign. He was soon after banished to the island of Elba, near Italy.

15. **D**. The British were not defeated by Napoleon during the Hundred Days. After his defeat in Russia, Napoleon was banished to the island of Elba near Italy. Not guarded too tightly, he escaped in 1815 and marched through France's countryside to gather supporters. He attempted to regain his Empire for about one hundred days. This attempt ended on June 18, 1815 when he lost the Battle of Waterloo. Napoleon was banished to the island of Saint Helena in the Atlantic. There, he died in 1821.

16. **A**. The Congress of Vienna was a meeting in Austria from 1814-1815. Led by Austrian Prince Klemens von Metternich, diplomats embraced ideas such as establishing a *balance of power* in Europe and restoring the *legitimacy* of the monarchs dethroned by Napoleon.

17. **A**. Fearful of revolutions similar to the one seen in France, coalitions such as the Holy Alliance and Metternich's Concert of Europe were formed. It was agreed that if an uprising broke out in one country, the members of the alliances would put it down. These alliances did not prevent the wars to come in the nineteenth century.

18. **A**. Known as the *Liberator*, Bolivar helped bring self-rule to South American countries including Colombia, Bolivia, Peru, and Venezuela.

19. **D**. Toussaint L'Ouverture led an uprising of slaves in Haiti that eventually led to its independence from France in 1804.

20. **A**. Mexican politician Benito Juárez presented liberal reforms in a movement called La Reforma. In the middle of the nineteenth century, he advocated for separation of church and state, and increased education for the poor.

21. **C**. Brazil received its independence from Portugal in 1822 through mostly peaceful measures. However, Portugal did not recognize their independence until 1825.

22. **B**. Just as the American Revolution inspired the French Revolution, the French Revolution inspired the Latin American ones. In addition, Enlightenment thought guided the people towards natural rights.

23. **B**. The 1789 *Declaration of the Rights of Man and of the Citizen* was a document similar to the American Declaration of Independence, which declared all men to be created equal. It promised to protect the natural rights of individuals.

24. **D**. Article 2 speaks of natural rights such as liberty and property. These ideas of John Locke were also adopted by the Declaration of Independence which fueled the American Revolution.

# 19th Century: Nationalism, the Industrial Revolution, and Imperialism

1. Nationalism is most likely to develop among
   A) those who are denied rights by an oppressor
   B) people who have a common culture or language
   C) the working class
   D) nobles, or wealthy landowners

2. The year 1848 was significant in Europe because
   A) communist forces took over Russia
   B) the Industrial Revolution began
   C) the Congress of Vienna adjourned
   D) revolutions spread throughout the continent

3. All of the following were important figures for the unification of Italy EXCEPT:
   A) Camillo di Cavour
   B) Giuseppe Garibaldi
   C) Giuseppe Mazzini
   D) Cosimo de' Medici

4. Which of the following became an idea widely preached by Otto von Bismarck?
   A) Authority should be used for practical reasons
   B) The proletariat should share the factors of production
   C) Independence for colonies is necessary
   D) Direct democracy is the most efficient form of government

5. Why did the Industrial Revolution begin in England?
   A) There were rich deposits of cotton
   B) There were abundant waterways for travel and power
   C) Europe's most capable scientists resided in London
   D) Imported goods from India could later be sold to neighboring countries

6. Steam-powered vessels and railroads
   A) were first used in Eastern Europe
   B) led to decreased farm output
   C) were pioneered by James Hargreaves
   D) fostered urbanization

7. All of the following were innovations first used during England's Agricultural Revolution EXCEPT:
   A) Seed drill
   B) Slash-and-burn farming
   C) Enclosures
   D) Crop rotation

8. Which of the following textile inventions came first?
   A) Flying shuttle
   B) Spinning mule
   C) Water frame
   D) Spinning jenny

9. A supporter of laissez-faire capitalism would believe that
   A) taxes should be increased on the wealthy
   B) minimum wage must be increased
   C) the government should not regulate big business
   D) the factors of production should be shared by the peasants

10. All of the following can be components of capitalism EXCEPT:
   A) Free-enterprise businesses
   B) Incentive for profit
   C) Classless societies
   D) Issuance of stock

11. *The Communist Manifesto* of Karl Marx and Friedrich Engels
   A) encouraged the upper classes to gain greater wealth
   B) advocated for the spread of Christianity
   C) supported the spread of monopolies
   D) encouraged the proletariat to rise in power

12. Whose philosophy reflected the belief that a government's actions would be deemed good if they provided for the happiness of many?
   A) Adam Smith
   B) Charles Darwin
   C) Jeremy Bentham
   D) Samuel Crompton

13. Massive Irish emigration in the middle of the nineteenth century was mostly a response to
   A) religious turmoil
   B) failure of the potato crop
   C) civil war
   D) a population boom

14. Darwin's theory of evolution was most controversial among
   A) heads of state
   B) members of the clergy
   C) scientists in South America
   D) Enlightenment scholars

15. Which country was originally founded as a penal colony?
   A) Australia
   B) Canada
   C) Ireland
   D) New Zealand

16. Ireland and Northern Ireland experienced violent clashes mostly concerning
   A) diplomatic treatment
   B) religion
   C) resistance to the Industrial Revolution
   D) support for World War I

17. Social Darwinism was used in the nineteenth century to justify
   A) absolute monarchy
   B) socialism
   C) the theory of evolution
   D) imperializing weaker nations

18. What work by Rudyard Kipling spoke about imperialists civilizing those seen as savages?
   A) *White Man's Burden*
   B) *The Ocean's Song*
   C) *A Sunset*
   D) *A Tale of Two Cities*

19. At the Berlin Conference
   A) the monarchs dethroned by Napoleon were restored
   B) an international peacekeeping organization was established
   C) African lands were divided among European powers
   D) revolutions in South America were outlawed

20. The Zulu chief Shaka helped Africa thrive in which modern-day region?
   A) Nigeria
   B) Congo
   C) South Africa
   D) Ethiopia

21. What was the immediate result of the Boer Wars?
   A) The expulsion of imperialists from South Africa
   B) An end to diamond excavation
   C) French implementation of apartheid
   D) British control in South Africa

22. The Crimean War proved that which Empire was gradually losing power?
   A) British
   B) Ottoman
   C) Mughal
   D) Safavid

23. What factor contributed most to the notion that India was the "jewel" in the British crown?
   A) It served as a buffer zone between both Hemispheres
   B) There was a large market to sell British goods
   C) Christianity was spread on a large scale
   D) New Indian architectural methods were brought back to Britain

24. What type of rumor triggered the Sepoy Mutiny?
   A) Taxes on imported tea
   B) Elimination of representation in Parliament
   C) Closing of the Ganges River
   D) Violation of religious practices

25. The Sepoy Rebellion and Opium Wars were both similar attempts to
   A) end foreign influences in a region
   B) limit the gap between the rich and poor
   C) decrease taxes
   D) dethrone monarchs

26. What territory did Britain gain from the Treaty of Nanjing that ended the first Opium War?
   A) Shanghai
   B) Hong Kong
   C) Beijing
   D) Xi'an

27. A sphere of influence is best defined as a
   A) region where a foreign power controls trade
   B) part of a country where religion is forbidden
   C) place where foreign trade is prohibited
   D) region where a local government has no power

28. Which of the following African countries remained independent from European imperialism by the end of the nineteenth century?
   A) Congo
   B) South Africa
   C) Ethiopia
   D) Mozambique

29. The United States implemented the Open Door Policy to
    A) limit British trade in Japan
    B) protect American trade interests in China
    C) allow the United States to gain control of the Chinese government
    D) end open immigration from China to the United States

30. Boxers were those Chinese peasants who
    A) supported the spread of Christianity
    B) profited from the opium trade
    C) disapproved of foreign influences
    D) assimilated to Western culture

31. The Meiji Era in Japan featured
    A) an end to the Emperor's rule
    B) massive emigration from the region
    C) resistance to Western culture
    D) the spread of railroads and factories

32. How did Japan and China differ regarding how they reacted to imperialism in the late nineteenth and early twentieth centuries?
    A) The Chinese embraced modernization
    B) The Japanese became imperialists
    C) China began to secure spheres of influences around the world
    D) The Japanese isolated themselves after the Age of Imperialism

Questions 33-34 are based on the map below.

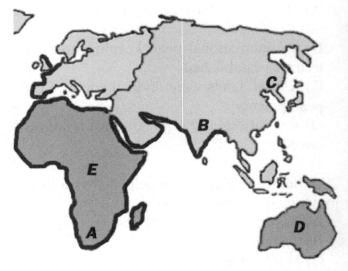

33. Which area was controlled by Belgium even decades after the Berlin Conference?
    A) A
    B) B
    C) C
    D) D
    E) E

34. Which area was ruled by the British Raj?
    A) A
    B) B
    C) C
    D) D
    E) E

35. Serfs existed in Russia until the nineteenth century when
    A) they were freed by Czar Alexander II
    B) their terms of service expired
    C) a serf uprising in Kiev led to their freedom
    D) they were liberated by the Ottoman Turks

## Answers and Explanations

1. **B.** Nationalism is a belief that one's loyalty rests with the people of a nation-state because of a common culture, heritage, set of beliefs, or interest. Typically, nationalism is accompanied by strong pride for one's nation-state/country.

2. **D.** In the bloody year of 1848, revolutions broke out all over Europe as nationalism and dissatisfaction with governments ran wild. France and modern-day Germany and Italy were greatly affected. People wanted more democracy, individual liberties, and improvements to working conditions.

3. **D.** Medici was powerful in Florence during the Renaissance.

4. **A.** Bismarck unified Germany with "Blood and Iron," as through war, Prussia won land. Bismarck used the diplomacy of *realpolitik*. This meant to rule with authority for practical, realistic, and material reasons…not for idealistic or moral ones.

5. **B.** England, though an island, has abundant natural resources such as coal and hydroelectric (water) power. Resources used to produce finished goods are called *factors of production*. These factors include capital, laborers, land/natural resources, and *entrepreneurships* (individual businesses). In addition, because it's an island on the English Channel, there are ample harbors suitable for trade. England also has rivers for domestic travel.

6. **D.** Urbanization, or the migration to cities, was enhanced by railroads that linked rural and urban (city) areas. Steam-powered vehicles, such as Robert Fulton's steamboat, were developed after the invention of James Watt's fuel-efficient steam engine.

7. **B.** Slash-and-burn farming goes back thousands of years. It meant that people cleared land for farms by burning trees. The ashes were then used as fertilizer.

8. **A.** John Kay's flying shuttle predated the other inventions, as it doubled the speed at which yarn could be spun. The other inventions spun even faster, or used water power.

9. **C.** In 1776 Adam Smith wrote *The Wealth of Nations* where he argued that the government should take its *hands off* the economy and permit a free market. This non-interference concept is called *laissez-faire*.

10. **C.** Socialism would involve a classless society of people. Owning a business (free enterprise), gaining profit, and the issuance of corporate stock can be components of capitalism.

11. **D.** Germans Karl Marx and Friedrich Engels wrote *The Communist Manifesto* in 1848 and criticized class struggle resulting from the Industrial Revolution. They encouraged the lower class, the proletariat, to rise up and eliminate all distinctions of classes. Marx favored a classless society.

12. **C**. Bentham believed in "the greatest happiness principle" where the government should provide the greatest good for the greatest number. This notion of the morality of actions being judged by their consequences is called utilitarianism. In other words, a government's actions would be deemed good if they provided for the happiness of many.

13. **B**. The potato famine of the mid-1840s caused a rift between Ireland and Great Britain, as the British did little to help the starving people of Ireland. An estimated one million people died during the famine. Many emigrated from the area. Ireland protested for home rule for decades.

14. **B**. Darwin made many of his observations at the Galapagos Islands off the west coast of South America. His theory of evolution was very controversial because it went against the creation teachings of the Bible.

15. **A**. Australia was founded as a penal colony, or a place for convicted criminals. After persecuting the local Aborigines, the British settled Australia, as well as neighboring New Zealand. In the early 1900s, both became dominions, meaning they could self-govern. Canada also became a dominion, earlier in 1867. Ireland received home rule much later.

16. **B**. It is important to note that Northern Ireland remains part of the United Kingdom. Ireland (Catholic) and Northern Ireland (Protestant) experienced much violence and conflict in the decades following independence. Religious strife even exists today.

17. **D**. Imperialism is when one powerful nation takes over a weaker territory and enforces their political, economic, and social ideals onto the conquered. Typically, this was rationalized through *Social Darwinism*, or a belief in "survival of the fittest."

18. **A**. The *White Man's Burden* was a poem in which Rudyard Kipling wrote about civilizing those seen as inferior. Remember: Assimilation is the process whereby the conquered adopts the imperializing nation's culture. Choices B and C are Victor Hugo poems, and choice D is the famous novel by Charles Dickens.

19. **C**. European nations assembled in Berlin, Germany to divide up the lands of Africa. Of course, no African leaders were present to object to this division. Britain and France came away with the most territory after the conference.

20. **C**. South Africa was thriving under the Zulu chief Shaka c1800. However, years later the Boers (Dutch settlers) took over the region. When diamonds and other riches were discovered there, the British swooped in.

21. **D**. Two Boer Wars were fought, the first from 1880-81, and the second from 1899-1902. The British used concentration camps against the Boers which upset other European nations. The British won, and the Union of South Africa remained in their hands until 1961.

22. **B**. The Russians hoped to gain land, as the Ottoman Empire was falling apart by 1854. Britain and France helped push back Russian advances. The Ottoman Empire continued to lose land in the Balkans (areas near Romania, Bulgaria, and Bosnia) before World War I. The once mighty Empire would become known as the "sick man of Europe."

23. **B.** Because India had a population hovering over 300 million, it was a great market for selling finished goods. Indian people were encouraged to purchase only British items. Eventually, India became known as the *"jewel in the crown,"* meaning it was the most valuable of all of the British colonial treasures. Besides its market, there were plenty of resources there as well.

24. **D.** A *sepoy* was an Indian soldier of Hindu or Muslim descent who was hired to fight for the British. The spark that triggered conflict was talk of the British using grease from meat in their firearm cartridges. Since soldiers bit open these cartridges when reloading, the grease would go against the religious dietary restrictions of the sepoys.

25. **A.** The first Opium War (there were two), saw Britain's powerful steamships and technologically advanced weapons defeat the Chinese who were resisting imperialism. The British also put down the Sepoy Mutiny, and strengthened their grip over India.

26. **B.** The First Opium War began in 1839, and the Treaty of Nanjing (Nanking) of 1842 gave Britain control of Hong Kong. Hong Kong would become a booming metropolis over the next century.

27. **A.** During the Age of Imperialism, conquering nations carved out a "sphere of influence," meaning they each began to control the trade within a piece of territory.

28. **C.** Ethiopia, under Menelik II, pushed back the Italian military to remain independent. Ethiopia would fall to Mussolini's Italy in the twentieth century. Liberia also remained independent in Africa after the Berlin Conference.

29. **B.** Generally, the Open Door Policy was created to protect American trading interests in China. The United States did not want to lose Chinese trade to other European countries, so it declared China open to all countries who wanted to trade. Of course, China could not object.

30. **C.** Boxers were Chinese people who wanted to drive out foreign imperialist nations. In addition, they resented Chinese conversions to Christianity. In 1900, they rebelled (in the Boxer Rebellion). Imperialist nations ended the uprising rather quickly. China would not rid itself of all foreign interests for another fifty years.

31. **D.** During the Meiji Era from 1868-1912, the Japanese embraced Western technology and modernized their factories and industry.

32. **B.** Japan began to model their government and economy after the West. Unlike the Chinese who were imperialized, the Japanese *became* imperialists. They fought several wars, including the Sino-Japanese War from 1894-5 and the Russo-Japanese War from 1904-5.

33. **E.** The King of Belgium controlled the Congo in Africa after the Berlin Conference. Congo wouldn't become independent until 1960.

34. **B.** Strict British rule in India, known as the *British Raj*, continued throughout the nineteenth and twentieth centuries. India received independence in 1947.

35. **A.** In the same century when slavery was abolished in much of the world, serfdom ended in Russia.

# World War I

1. Which of the following was the IMMEDIATE cause for World War I?
   A) Militarism in France
   B) Forming of Alliances
   C) Weakening of the Ottoman Empire
   D) Assassination of Archduke Franz Ferdinand

2. Which of the following was NOT a nation in the Triple Alliance?
   A) Italy
   B) Germany
   C) Austria-Hungary
   D) Russia

3. What was the Schlieffen Plan of World War I?
   A) Russia's attempt to control the Western Front
   B) Germany's hope to take over France, and then move east
   C) Austria-Hungary's plan to win a war on two fronts simultaneously
   D) Britain's desire to fight only on the Western Front

4. Why did Russia drop out of World War I?
   A) Revolutionaries removed them from the conflict
   B) The Russians ran out of provisions and surrendered
   C) Germany had taken over St. Petersburg
   D) Czar Nicholas II pulled the country out of the war due to low morale

5. What impact did the sinking of the *Lusitania* and the Zimmermann Telegram have on World War I?
   A) Both put into question freedom of the seas
   B) They were instrumental in bringing the United States into the war
   C) Both were conflicts caused by Great Britain
   D) The events directly led to an armistice

6. Which innovation of World War I proved to be the most controversial?
   A) Tanks
   B) Trench warfare
   C) Mustard gas
   D) Machine guns

7. Which of the following was NOT a part of Woodrow Wilson's Fourteen Points?
   A) Freedom of the seas
   B) Fair trade
   C) Border security
   D) Territorial expansion

8. One weakness of the League of Nations was
   A) United States dominance within the League
   B) German involvement in the organization
   C) a lack of an army to enforce peace
   D) veto power of the five permanent nations

9. All of the following leaders were part of the Big Four of the post-World War I peace process EXCEPT:
   A) Georges Clemenceau
   B) David Lloyd George
   C) Vittorio Orlando
   D) Kaiser Wilhelm

10. Which of the following was NOT a punishment handed out to Germany in the Treaty of Versailles?
   A) The loss of overseas colonies
   B) A limiting of the size of its army
   C) War reparations to a sum of 33 billion dollars
   D) The division of Germany into sections controlled by the Allies

11. After World War I, which country was established from the former Austria-Hungary?
   A) Finland
   B) Ukraine
   C) Turkey
   D) Czechoslovakia

12. Mustafa Kemal Atatürk's Republic of Turkey became a
   A) state governed by Islamic Law
   B) westernized country
   C) republic still controlled by the Ottoman Empire
   D) country isolated from European trade

13. During and after World War I, the Armenian population in the former Ottoman Empire
   A) became victims of starvation
   B) renounced their faith
   C) immigrated to the Holy Land
   D) revolted in an attempt to bring back the Ottoman state

Questions 14-15 are based on the selection below.

"The territories which were ceded to Germany in accordance with the Preliminaries of Peace signed at Versailles on February 26, 1871, and the Treaty of Frankfort of May 10, 1871, are restored to French sovereignty as from the date of the Armistice of November 11, 1918."
   – Article 51 of the Treaty of Versailles

14. What conflict of the nineteenth century is being referenced in the above document?
   A) Sepoy Mutiny
   B) Franco-Prussian War
   C) Seven Weeks' War
   D) Boer War

15. Which specific region is referenced in the above document?
   A) Paris
   B) Alsace-Lorraine
   C) Normandy
   D) Marseille

## Answers and Explanations

1. **D**. The spark that started the war was the assassination of Archduke Franz Ferdinand who was shot by Serbian nationalist Gavrilo Princip in Sarajevo on June 28, 1914. Serbia was one of several nations who broke away from the "sick man" of Europe...the Ottoman Empire.

2. **D**. Russia was part of the Triple-Entente, and later the Allies of World War I.

3. **B**. The early German strategy was called the Schlieffen Plan. Its goal was to swiftly defeat France, and then move eastward to defeat Russia. This never happened.

4. **A**. Russia had internal problems to deal with during World War I, as the Bolshevik Revolution spread throughout the country.

5. **B**. The *Lusitania* was a passenger ship that was sunk by a German submarine (U-boat). This put into question freedom of the seas in the Atlantic. The Zimmermann Telegram unveiled a plot for Germany to align with Mexico and target the United States.

6. **C**. A German innovation that was soon used by the Allies, chemical weapons were common in the Great War. Gas masks were used by both sides to prevent respiratory failure. The use of chemical gas has become, even to this day, a controversial weapon of war.

7. **D**. In a 1918 speech, Wilson addressed issues of fair trade, freedom of the seas, treatment of the imperialized, an international peace-keeping organization, and constructing new borders.

8. **C**. Most important of Wilson's Fourteen Points was his last point, which was to create an international peace-keeping organization. This would become the League of Nations. Unlike today's United Nations, the League could not raise an army to enforce peace. In addition, the United States did not enter the League. Choice D would be true of the United Nations.

9. **D**. Wilhelm, the leader of Germany, was not a part of the Big Four. The Big Four who helped influence the Treaty of Versailles were Woodrow Wilson of the United States, David Lloyd George of Britain, Georges Clemenceau of France, and Vittorio Orlando of Italy.

10. **D**. Germany would become divided into East and West Germany…but that was after World War II. The other choices reflect punishments dished out by the Treaty of Versailles. Many historians believe that the severe punishments of the Treaty of Versailles were a cause for World War II.

11. **D**. Austria-Hungary became Austria, Hungary, and Czechoslovakia. Some land would eventually become Yugoslavia.

12. **B**. Turkey's independence movement was led by Mustafa Kemal Atatürk. He became the first president of the Republic of Turkey in 1923, and transformed the country into a secular state (not controlled by Islam). He helped bring women equality under the law, and encouraged them to give up their veils and dress in Western clothes. Women also received full political rights, including suffrage.

13. **A**. Before World War I, the Christian Armenian population demanded rights within the Ottoman Empire. They were met with a fierce military resistance. Many were killed. Then, during and after World War I, Armenians suffered deportation, starvation, forced marches, torture, and execution. An estimated 1-1.5 million people were killed in the atrocities. The killing ended in 1923. Though considered by many to be genocide, the Turkish government denied such claims.

14. **B**. In the Franco-Prussian War of 1870-71, Prussia (later becoming a unified Germany) received land from France.

15. **B**. Alsace-Lorraine was a region received by Germany after the Franco-Prussian War. France would get the land back after World War I.

# The Russian Revolution and Joseph Stalin

1. The pogroms were
   A) a violent form of Anti-Semitism
   B) organized demonstrations against the czar
   C) reforms within the Eastern Orthodox Church
   D) forced collectivization measures against Ukrainian farmers

2. Bloody Sunday was a response to
   A) Jews migrating to the Russian capital
   B) women protesting for fair bread prices
   C) workers demonstrating for labor rights
   D) anti-war protests during the Russo-Japanese War

3. Put the following events of the Russian Revolution into chronological order:

   A. Removal of Rasputin
   B. Provisional Government takes power
   C. Russian Civil War
   D. November Revolution

   A) A-B-C-D
   B) C-A-B-D
   C) C-A-D-B
   D) A-B-D-C

4. Which of the following Russian leaders preached "peace, land, and bread"?
   A) Joseph Stalin
   B) Vladimir Lenin
   C) Czar Nicholas II
   D) Grigori Rasputin

5. What did the Treaty of Brest-Litovsk do?
   A) Officially end Romanov rule
   B) Divide land between the peasants
   C) End the Russian Civil War
   D) Allow Russia to drop out of World War I

6. Who led the Red Army during the Russian Civil War?
   A) Leon Trotsky
   B) Joseph Stalin
   C) Alexander Kerensky
   D) Nicholas Romanov

7. Why were kulaks most upset with Lenin's ideas?
   A) They were proponents of democracy
   B) As wealthy Russians, they resented land redistribution
   C) They supported Eastern Orthodox Christianity
   D) As nationalistic Russians, they wanted to continue fighting in World War I

8. Lenin's New Economic Policy (NEP)
   A) permitted some capitalism and profit
   B) eliminated all shopkeepers
   C) limited the amount of grain one could harvest
   D) was best described as laissez-faire capitalism

9. The Union of Soviet Socialist Republics was a
   A) weak confederation where sovereign states had greater power than Moscow
   B) territory which included all land from East Germany and Czechoslovakia
   C) centralized state headquartered in Russia but controlling neighboring regions
   D) fragmented group of independent states

10. Totalitarianism refers to a government where
    A) the people share the total means of production
    B) aspects of public and private life are controlled by the state
    C) propaganda techniques are facilitated by private companies
    D) one class of people has all of the power

11. The spreading of Russian culture throughout the Soviet Union was known as
    A) Stalinism
    B) Russification
    C) Totalitarianism
    D) Bolshevism

12. Gulags were best described as
    A) living residences for government dignitaries
    B) meeting places for Soviet officials
    C) places of worship
    D) Soviet labor camps

13. What religious ideology was favored by Joseph Stalin's government?
    A) Atheism
    B) Judaism
    C) Roman Catholicism
    D) Eastern Orthodox

14. Which best explains the type of economy favored by Joseph Stalin?
    A) Command
    B) Capitalism
    C) Free-enterprise
    D) Self-sufficiency

15. Why was Stalin's first Five-Year Plan unattainable?
    A) Russia lacked the resources to achieve industrialization
    B) World War I had destroyed most Russian factories
    C) There was a shortage of industrial workers
    D) Stalin set very high quotas for industry

16. During the 1930s, how was Joseph Stalin able to maintain a favorable image among the Russian people?
    A) Victories in foreign wars gave him prestige
    B) A massive propaganda campaign provided only positive images of Stalin
    C) Collectivization of farms brought an end to hunger
    D) An economic boom after the first Five-Year Plan led to prosperity

17. The Great Purge refers to Joseph Stalin's use of
A) industrialization to modernize the Soviet Union
B) force to remove those seen as traitors
C) socialism to stabilize the economy
D) propaganda to control public opinion

Questions 18-20 are based on the selection below.

"History will not forgive revolutionaries for procrastinating when they could be victorious today (and they certainly will be victorious today)… If we seize power today, we seize it not in opposition to the Soviets but on their behalf. The seizure of power is the business of the uprising; its political purpose will become clear after the seizure." - November, 1917

18. Which best describes the definition of a "Soviet"?
   A) A local council of workers
   B) Supporters of the Czar
   C) Clergy in the Eastern Orthodox Church
   D) Proponents of capitalism

19. Who is the author of the above speech?
   A) Vladimir Lenin
   B) Alexander Kerensky
   C) Joseph Stalin
   D) Czar Nicholas II

20. What event took place after the seizure of power so the "political purpose" could be carried out?
   A) World War I
   B) Bloody Sunday
   C) March Revolution
   D) Russian Civil War

## Answers and Explanations

1. **A**. Under Czar Alexander III, there was a hope to unify Russian culture. This meant persecution of the many Jews who lived in the country. Pogroms were organized massacres that targeted them. Jews were also removed to an area of Russia known as the pale of settlement. Anti-Semitism caused many to emigrate from Russia during the early twentieth century.

2. **C**. When thousands of workers protested for labor rights in St. Petersburg, the Czar's Imperial Guard fired on the crowd. The backlash to this event led to the creation of a Russian parliament known as the Duma.

3. **D**. Rasputin came to power, and was executed in 1916. The Czar was overthrown and replaced by the Provisional Government in March of 1917. Next, Lenin and the Bolsheviks came to power in November of 1917. Finally, the Russian Civil War was fought from 1918-1921.

4. **B**. Lenin hoped to bring the Russian people *"peace, land, and bread."* He and the Bolsheviks overthrew the Provisional Government to gain control of Russia. To make sure the Czar's supporters didn't restore him to the throne, the entire royal family was executed in 1918. The capital of Russia was soon moved from St. Petersburg to Moscow.

5. **D**. The 1918 Treaty of Brest-Litovsk allowed Russia to drop out of World War I. Russia gave up western land to achieve this.

6. **A**. In the Russian Civil War, Leon Trotsky led the Bolshevik Red Army against the anti-Bolshevik White Army. Between the fighting, famine, and disease, more Russians were killed in this war than in World War I. Estimates range from 10-15 million. The Red Army won the war, and the communists continued to rule Russia.

7. **B**. Lenin began to divide up all of the farms and factories amongst the people. This upset the many landowning *kulaks*, or wealthier Russians.

8. **A**. After the Russian Civil War, Lenin set up NEP. NEP permitted some capitalism, as shopkeepers were allowed to keep small profits. However, the government remained in control of most production in the factory system.

9. **C**. In 1922, Russia and surrounding lands such as Ukraine and Belarus became the Union of Soviet Socialist Republics (USSR). It can also be called the Soviet Union. This enormous area extended into northern Asia.

10. **B**. Joseph Stalin was a harsh dictator who ruled through totalitarianism. Totalitarianism occurs when a government not only controls the economic and political lives of the people, but their social rights as well.

11. **B**. A movement called Russification attempted to expand the Russian culture and language to areas far away from Moscow.

12. **D**. Those who went against Stalin were either killed or sent to a labor camp known as a gulag.

13. **A**. Stalin controlled production, the media, the economy, and everything else under the Soviet sun. Churches were destroyed, and atheism (rejection of a belief in God) was supported. Religion was considered a threat to Soviet power.

14. **A**. Stalin commanded the economy, meaning he made all regulations for agriculture and industry.

15. **D**. Regarding industry, Stalin made a series of Five-Year Plans which aimed to modernize the Soviet Union, as it lagged behind other European countries. The plan looked to produce raw materials such as coal and iron, and extend railway lines, electricity, and communication networks. Production from factories increased, but they never met the impossible quotas that Stalin set out to achieve.

16. **B**. Through fear and immense propaganda (biased media coverage, posters, school curriculum, speeches, and parades), Stalin *indoctrinated* the people of Russia. This meant that his views were accepted as truth. All opposition was silenced.

17. **B**. To purge means to remove or kill. Stalin's secret police rounded up suspected enemies of the state and they were either murdered or shipped to a gulag. The Great Purge targeted government officials in the Communist Party and peasants who were seen as enemies of the state. After unfair trials, most were executed. The killings peaked from 1937-38.

18. **A**. The term soviet would go on to mean someone from the Soviet Union. In this case, before the Soviet Union was formed, it means local councils, or assemblies, of workers.

19. **A**. The speech was given in November of 1917, amidst the November Revolution. The leader of that revolution was Vladimir Lenin.

20. **D**. In order for the Soviets to maintain power, the Russian Civil War was fought. With the Bolsheviks victorious, they continued communist rule over Russia, and later formed the Soviet Union.

# Fascism, World War II, and the Holocaust

1. Which of the following best explains the principles of fascism?

A) A socialist economy combined with a democratic political system

B) A dictatorship that promotes nationalism through military force

C) A free enterprise economy that promotes democracy

D) A dictatorship with a socialist economy

2. What mistake made by the Weimar Republic was MOST disastrous to the German economy?

A) Raising interest rates

B) Lowering tariffs

C) Increasing the amount of money in circulation

D) Refusing to create a central banking authority

3. Which of the following had the LEAST significant impact on the rise of fascism in Italy?

A) A fear of communism

B) Economic discontent

C) Nationalism

D) Loss of overseas colonies

4. The Lateran Pacts favored which religion in Italy?

A) Eastern Orthodox

B) Presbyterianism

C) Roman Catholicism

D) Lutheranism

5. Which of the following was NOT a cause for the rise of Adolf Hitler?

A) German support for the Treaty of Versailles

B) A fear of communism

C) Weaknesses of the Weimar Republic

D) German nationalism

6. Francisco Franco advocated for which of the following types of governments for Spain?

A) Fascism

B) Communism

C) Democracy

D) Aristocracy

7. What impact did Joseph Goebbels have on the Third Reich?

A) He developed new military strategies

B) His use of propaganda escalated support for Hitler

C) He was responsible for the Final Solution

D) He was instrumental in removing nationalism from Germany

8. *Lebensraum* referred to the German need to

A) segregate Jews from the general population

B) promote the master race within government

C) acquire more territory for Germany to expand

D) militarize for naval defense

9. The Gestapo in Nazi Germany was responsible for
   A) arresting suspected enemies of state
   B) expanding freedom of speech
   C) declaring war on foreign countries
   D) censoring the ideas of Friedrich Nietzsche

10. The Tripartite Pact established the
   A) Axis Powers
   B) Atlantic Charter
   C) annexation of Austria
   D) alliance between Germany and the Soviet Union

11. Which of the following was NOT a territory taken by Adolf Hitler?
   A) Austria
   B) Sudetenland
   C) Rhineland
   D) Manchester

12. An example of appeasement before World War II was
   A) Mussolini conquering Ethiopia
   B) the founding of the Axis Powers
   C) the Munich Conference
   D) Japan's attack on Pearl Harbor

13. Which of the following is true of the Nazi-Soviet nonaggression pact?
   A) It was the first time that people of German and Russian heritage were Allies
   B) Hitler would break the pact and invade the Soviet Union
   C) The pact did not cause any alarm in the Western world
   D) The Soviets joined the Axis Powers for the duration of the war

14. In the year 1934, who of the following was NOT yet the leader of the country they are paired with?
   A) Japan – Emperor Hirohito
   B) Ethiopia – Haile Selassie
   C) Soviet Union – Joseph Stalin
   D) People's Republic of China – Mao Zedong

15. In *Mein Kampf*, Adolf Hitler advocated for the
   A) elimination of capitalist classes
   B) promotion of a master race of Aryans
   C) final solution of the Holocaust
   D) spread of communism in Western Europe

16. The Kellogg-Briand Pact and the Washington Naval Conference can both be considered
   A) a successful remedy for war in the twentieth century
   B) failed attempts to bring a lasting peace after World War I
   C) ways of appeasing Adolf Hitler
   D) failed solutions for the post-World War I economic crisis

17. Put the following events of World War II into chronological order:

   A. Attack on Pearl Harbor
   B. D-Day
   C. Hitler invades Poland
   D. Blitzkrieg of London

   A) A-B-C-D
   B) C-D-B-A
   C) A-B-D-C
   D) C-D-A-B

18. In defeating Japan in World War II, the United States used all of the following strategies EXCEPT:
   A) The use of atomic weapons
   B) Island-hopping in the Pacific Ocean
   C) A mainland invasion of Japan
   D) Diplomacy with the Soviets

19. The Atlantic Charter was an agreement
   A) which outlawed war between Germany and the Soviet Union
   B) that sought to stabilize the world through peaceful measures
   C) for the United States to join the League of Nations
   D) which outlawed freedom of the seas

20. Why can the Yalta Conference be considered to be the beginning of the Cold War?
   A) It led to direct fighting between the United States and the Soviet Union
   B) It formally led to a permanent divide between Poland and the Soviet Union
   C) Joseph Stalin expanded communist control over Eastern Europe
   D) Harry Truman received false Soviet promises for free elections in Poland

21. Which of the following persecutions of Jews occurred first?
   A) Removal to the Warsaw Ghetto
   B) Nuremberg Laws
   C) Kristallnacht
   D) Final Solution

22. During ghetto life, Jews resisted in the greatest numbers by
   A) arming themselves in rebellion
   B) smuggling necessities such as food and religious materials
   C) contacting foreign embassies for military support
   D) sabotaging the German war effort

23. The Nazis violently targeted all of the following people during World War II EXCEPT:
   A) Jews
   B) Gypsies
   C) Mentally ill
   D) Aryans

24. Zyklon B was a chemical most associated with
   A) extermination camps
   B) removing vegetation from battlefields
   C) burning civilian villages
   D) destroying railroad lines between countries

25. Literature from Elie Wiesel and Anne Frank both
   A) gave horrific accounts of life in concentration camps
   B) provided primary source accounts of the Holocaust
   C) introduced insights which led to the end of Anti-Semitism
   D) were cited as evidence at the Nuremberg Trials

26. The Nuremberg Trials were concerned with
A) holding individuals responsible for the horrors of the Holocaust
B) deciding the fate of satellite nations in the early years of the Cold War
C) levying monetary war reparations against Germany
D) creating a collective security organization after World War II

Questions 26-27 are based on the selection below.

"WE THE PEOPLES OF THE UNITED NATIONS DETERMINED
• to save succeeding generations from the scourge of war, which twice in our lifetime has brought untold sorrow to mankind, and
• to reaffirm faith in fundamental human rights, in the dignity and worth of the human person, in the equal rights of men and women and of nations large and small, and
• to establish conditions under which justice and respect for the obligations arising from treaties and other sources of international law can be maintained, and
• to promote social progress and better standards of life in larger freedom…"
– Preamble to the United Nations Charter

27. Which events of the twentieth century had the greatest influence on this charter?
A) World War I and World War II
B) The Holocaust and World War II
C) Use of atomic bombs in World War II and the creation of the Hydrogen Bomb
D) World War I and the Bolshevik Revolution

28. Which philosophical movement's ideas are visible in the charter?
A) Scientific Revolution
B) Existentialism
C) Enlightenment
D) Social Darwinism

## Answers and Explanations

1. **B.** Fascism became popular in certain European countries between the World Wars. It is a political ideology where a dictator promotes nationalism under the threat of extensive military force. A fascist dictator controls nearly all aspects of life within a nation. Fascism grew out of discontent and desperation in the years following World War I.

2. **C.** In Germany, the new democratic Weimar Republic attempted to handle their economic problems by printing more money. This devalued the currency, as immense inflation occurred. This further made the economy spiral out of control.

3. **D.** Mussolini was a fascist dictator in Italy from 1922 through most of World War II. He was able to rise because there was extreme discontent with the economic depression following World War I, a fear of a workers' communist revolt, and immense nationalism among the people.

4. **C.** Mussolini made Roman Catholicism the favored religion of Italy as per the Lateran Pacts (agreements with the Church).

5. **A.** The harsh punishments of the Treaty of Versailles were resented by the German people, and the treaty itself is considered by many historians to be a contributing factor for the rise of fascism in Germany.

6. **A.** Spain became engaged in a civil war in 1936 when Francisco Franco's fascist Nationalist Army attempted to seize power. Hitler and Mussolini both supported Franco, and the Spanish government was overthrown in 1939. Franco was in office until 1975. Spain gradually moved to democracy after his death.

7. **B.** With the help of Propaganda Minister Joseph Goebbels, a "big lie" was created through radio, posters, school control, speeches, and parades. Everywhere, flags with the Nazi swastika symbol could be seen. Literature that went against Nazi ideals was banned or burned.

8. **C.** *Lebensraum* was an appeal to Germans to increase the "living space" of the country.

9. **A.** Enemies were targeted through both Heinrich Himmler's military, the SS (Schutzstaffel), and the Gestapo (secret state police).

10. **A.** Under the pact, Germany, Japan, and Italy formed an alliance known as the Axis Powers.

11. **D.** Hitler never conquered Britain or took Manchester. Germany remilitarized the Rhineland on its western border (which was in violation of the Treaty of Versailles). In addition, Hitler annexed (added to Germany) Austria through a process called Anschluss. Hitler also wanted the Sudetenland, an area of Czechoslovakia where the people spoke German. He was given this territory at the 1938 Munich Conference.

12. **C.** At the Munich Conference, British Prime Minister Neville Chamberlain said that the transfer of the Sudetenland to Hitler would give the world "peace in our time." He was wrong, as it only made Hitler hungry for more. The Munich Conference is an example of appeasement, or meeting the aggressor's demands to keep peace.

13. **B**. In 1939, the Soviets and Germans agreed not to attack each other. Because both powers were natural enemies, many were doubtful this agreement would last. It didn't. However Hitler would suffer a similar fate as Napoleon. The harsh climate made the Russian land nearly impossible to conquer.

14. **D**. Mao Zedong did not officially become the leader of the People's Republic of China until 1949.

15. **B**. Hitler wrote *Mein Kampf* (My Struggle) from prison a decade before his rise. In the book, he explained how he thought Germany should be governed. Furthermore, he spoke of the German *master race* of Aryans, whom he believed were superior to Jews and other minorities in Germany.

16. **B**. In between the World Wars: The Washington Naval Conference of 1921 saw the major powers agree to limit naval arms. The Kellogg-Briand Pact of 1928 renounced war as a form of national policy. However, peace would not last.

17. **D**. Invasion of Poland (1939), Blitzkrieg of London (1940), Pearl Harbor (1941), D-Day (1944).

18. **C**. The dropping of the atomic bomb prevented an invasion of Japan. Earlier, the United States "island hopped" from places such as Midway, Iwo Jima, and Okinawa. The Soviets agreed to enter the Pacific theater in 1945.

19. **B**. The United Nations grew out of the Atlantic Charter of 1941, where Winston Churchill and Franklin Roosevelt agreed to stabilize the world with peace once the war ended. The US, Soviet Union, France, Britain, and China would be the Five Permanent Nations with veto power. Unlike the League of Nations, the UN can assemble peacekeeping troops. Also, unlike the League, the US joined the UN.

20. **C**. The Yalta Conference gave the Soviet Union control over much of Eastern Europe. Though the Soviets promised free elections, these promises were empty, as the nations were turned into satellites. It can be said that Yalta was the start of the Cold War. Choice D, though almost correct, isn't, as Stalin promised this to Truman later during the war. President Franklin Roosevelt was present at Yalta.

21. **B**. Before the later events of the Holocaust, Jews were denied basic freedoms with the 1935 Nuremberg Laws. Kristallnacht translates to "night of broken glass." On November 9, 1938 Nazi soldiers attacked Jews, their homes, and their synagogues. Thousands of Jewish establishments were burned and vandalized all over Germany and Austria. After Jews were later removed to ghettos, the Final Solution, or genocide, was the measure which occurred last.

22. **B**. Like the pogroms of Russia c1900, German Jews were forced to live in reserved areas (mostly in Poland). The Nazis sealed the borders of these ghettos leading to starvation and disease. Still, Jews were able to smuggle in necessities such as food, and religious materials.

23. **D**. Aryans were members of the master race. The Final Solution was genocide, or the methodical killing of an entire group of people. Those seen as undesirable or inferior to the master race of Aryans were targeted. Jews, Gypsies, homosexuals, the mentally ill, and others were murdered.

24. **A**. The killing of the Final Solution was done in concentration camps and extermination camps. Many died in concentration camps through slave labor. Later in the war, extermination camps such as Auschwitz in Poland, were used for the purpose of killing. A chemical named Zyklon B was used to murder Jews in showers.

25. **B**. Ellie Wiesel's *Night*, and the *Diary of Anne Frank* were primary accounts of the horrors of the Holocaust. Wiesel explained life at Auschwitz, an infamous concentration camp. Anne Frank wrote about her experiences hiding out in Amsterdam, Netherlands. She and her family were captured at the end of the war.

26. **A**. After the war ended, the world looked for accountability regarding the Holocaust. In the first of a series of trials, 22 Nazis were charged with war crimes. 12 were sentenced to death. Hundreds of Nazi officers associated with concentration or extermination camps were never tried for crimes against humanity.

27. **A**. The first statement talks of the scourge of war which happened twice in a lifetime. This sentence is referring to the two World Wars of the twentieth century.

28. **C**. One can see Enlightenment rhetoric in the excerpt, including ideas of human rights and freedom.

# The Cold War, Korean and Vietnam Wars

1. Which of the following was true of the Soviet Union?
   A) It wanted to contain communism
   B) It hoped to keep Germany divided
   C) It was led by Nikita Khrushchev during the early 1940s
   D) It combined democracy with a socialistic economy

2. The Truman Doctrine can best be described as
   A) a policy that looked to spread communism
   B) billions of dollars in aid for NATO nations
   C) military aid to those resisting communism
   D) a plan to deploy troops to countries in need

3. What was the purpose behind the Marshall Plan?
   A) Forcing communist nations to adopt capitalism
   B) Creating a plan for nuclear proliferation
   C) Bolstering America's arsenal after World War II
   D) Strengthening the free nations of Europe

4. George Kennan's policy of containment can best be described as the
   A) easing of tensions with the Soviet Union
   B) spending of money on municipal infrastructure
   C) forming of alliances against fascist aggression
   D) preventing of the spread of communism

5. The Berlin Airlift was an American and British response to the
   A) denial of free elections in East Germany
   B) Soviet Union's blockade of West Berlin
   C) forming of the Warsaw Pact
   D) limiting of civil liberties in East Germany

6. Which of the following nations was NOT a member of NATO c1980?
   A) East Germany
   B) France
   C) Italy
   D) Spain

7. The Soviet Union's launching of Sputnik led directly to
   A) extended American investments in nuclear weaponry
   B) an increase in funding for scientific education in the United States
   C) the shipping of US missiles to Turkey
   D) the deployment of US troops to the Berlin Wall

8. The outcome of the Bay of Pigs Invasion was significant because it
   A) temporarily removed Fidel Castro from power
   B) eliminated communist influence in Latin America
   C) intensified poor US-Cuban relations
   D) strengthened the international prestige of President John F. Kennedy

9. Which of the following was NOT associated with the Cuban Missile Crisis?
    A) Diplomacy of détente
    B) Soviet missiles arriving in shipments to Cuba
    C) A threatened United States invasion of Cuba
    D) Brinkmanship

10. The Soviet-Afghan War and the Iranian Revolution proved that
    A) containment was an ineffective foreign policy
    B) the United Nations could maintain world peace
    C) the Cold War had implications in the Middle East
    D) westernization was universally popular

11. What impact did glasnost and perestroika have on the Soviet Union?
    A) Both policies helped lead to the fall of communism
    B) Mikhail Gorbachev strengthened his grip over the country
    C) Criticism of the government led to many arrests and deportations
    D) The elimination of clergy positions led to a weakening of religion

12. The intent of the failed August Coup of 1991 was to
    A) tear down the Berlin Wall in Germany
    B) decrease the Soviet Union's dependence on foreign oil
    C) begin administering the policy of glasnost
    D) affirm communist rule in the Soviet Union

13. The CIS (Commonwealth of Independent States) became a
    A) communist federation
    B) loose union of former Soviet republics
    C) UN controlled area
    D) political stronghold for Mikhail Gorbachev

14. After the Fall of Communism, the map of Europe changed. Which country became "re-unified"?
    A) Germany
    B) Czechoslovakia
    C) Yugoslavia
    D) Romania

15. Who of the following was associated with the liberation of Poland from communist rule?
    A) Slobodan Milosevic
    B) Boris Yeltsin
    C) Lech Walesa
    D) Leonid Brezhnev

16. In the 1990s, which regional tension was experienced in Bosnia-Herzegovina?
    A) religious and political conflict
    B) economic upheaval
    C) the rise of communism
    D) collectivization and famine

17. Which country is divided at the 38th parallel?
    A) Korea
    B) Vietnam
    C) Laos
    D) Cambodia

18. The Domino Theory was used by the United States to justify
   A) stopping the spread of communism in Asia
   B) ending the war in Vietnam
   C) preventing the United Nations from deploying troops
   D) putting an end to westernization in the Middle East

19. Which country controlled Vietnam before Dien Bien Phu fell in 1954?
   A) Britain
   B) Spain
   C) United States
   D) France

20. Put the following events of the Vietnam War into chronological order:

   A. Gulf of Tonkin Resolution
   B. Tet Offensive
   C. Paris Peace Accords
   D. Saigon becomes Ho Chi Minh City

   A) A-B-C-D
   B) A-C-B-D
   C) B-A-D-C
   D) B-A-C-D

21. The Khmer Rouge government under Pol Pot
   A) decreased the communist influence in Cambodia
   B) was responsible for inflicting genocide
   C) helped remove Ho Chi Minh from power
   D) aided Ferdinand Marcos and the Philippines in their fight for independence

Questions 22-23 are based on the selection below.

"But this secret, swift, and extraordinary build-up of communist missiles - in an area well known to have a special and historical relationship to the United States and the nations of the Western Hemisphere…is a deliberately provocative and unjustified change in the status quo which cannot be accepted by this country if our courage and our commitments are ever to be trusted again by either friend or foe.
"The 1930s taught us a clear lesson: Aggressive conduct, if allowed to grow unchecked and unchallenged, ultimately leads to war."
   – President John F. Kennedy, October 22, 1962

22. Which lesson does Kennedy believe was taught in the 1930s?
   A) appeasement is not a suitable foreign policy
   B) containment of aggressors produces poor results
   C) collective security measures can never succeed
   D) Soviet expansion should always be kept in check

23. Which of the following was part of the solution to the Cuban Missile Crisis?
   A) A planned attack of the Soviet mainland
   B) An airlift of aid to the Cuban people
   C) An invasion at the Bay of Pigs
   D) A blockade of Cuba to prevent military shipments

## Answers and Explanations

1. **B.** The Soviet Union wanted to: 1. Spread communism. 2. Control Eastern Europe to protect Soviet borders. 3. Keep Germany divided.

2. **C.** The Doctrine gave military aid (no troops) to countries resisting communism. Greece and Turkey took advantage of this aid.

3. **D.** US Secretary of State George Marshall's plan was a strategy to give economic aid to countries that were not communist. The idea was to make countries stronger, and less susceptible to communist takeovers. About $12.5 billion was given to nations all over Europe.

4. **D.** The foreign policy of the United States during the Cold War was containment. US diplomat George Kennan coined this term which meant preventing the spread of communism. This was typically done by forming alliances with weaker countries to fend off communist aggression. Containment is the opposite of appeasement (giving in to what the aggressor wants). Containment is also the most important term of the Cold War. Why did the US get involved in Korea? Containment. Why did the US send troops to Vietnam? Containment. Why did the US spend so much money on the military? Containment.

5. **B.** Soviet leader Joseph Stalin, wanting to keep Germany divided, blockaded the highway and rail resources coming into West Berlin (the non-communist side). He hoped this would make West Berlin dependent upon him and his satellites for supplies. However, the US and Great Britain sent 277,000 flights full of food and necessities for the German people. A furious Stalin thought the airlift might lead to war with the US. But, as with everything else in the Cold War, direct conflict was avoided.

6. **A.** East Germany was in the Warsaw Pact, West Germany was in NATO. Think of NATO (North Atlantic Treaty Organization) and the Warsaw Pact (Communist Bloc) as the two gangs of the Cold War.

7. **B.** In 1957, the Soviets successfully launched a satellite named Sputnik into space. Not only did this make Americans nervous about Soviet technology, but it gave the US a feeling of inferiority. The result of Sputnik's launch was an American increase of spending on education and science. In 1969, the US would win the space race to the moon.

8. **C.** Fidel Castro helped overthrow dictator Fulgencio Batista at the end of the Cuban Revolution in 1959. Castro soon took over Cuba's economy and ruled firmly over the people. He eliminated all opposition. President John F. Kennedy saw Castro as a threat to political and economic security in the region. Therefore, the US supported a rebellion led by Cuban exiles. They were defeated at the Bay of Pigs in Cuba. Not only did the US sponsor the failed rebellion, but the event strengthened the legitimacy of Castro.

Castro would soon become one of the Soviet Union's most important communist allies.

9. **A**. The Cuban Missile Crisis was the opposite of détente. Détente meant the easing of Cold War tensions. The Cuban Missile Crisis almost resulted in war. However, the Soviet Union eventually removed their missiles from Cuba after the US promised not to invade. The US also agreed to remove missiles of their own from Turkey.

10. **C**. The Soviets looked to spread communism in Afghanistan, but could never take over the country. In addition, the Iranian Revolution was fueled by anti-Western sentiment.

11. **A**. With Mikhail Gorbachev leading the Soviet Union, there was a new outlook that ultimately hurt communism. After he took office in 1985, the Soviet Union adopted two major policies: 1. *Glasnost* , or an openness that allowed people to voice their views on government. 2. *Perestroika*, or the restructuring of economics, which included some private business ownership.

12. **D**. By 1991, communism was falling all over Europe. Gorbachev lost his legitimacy, as the people supported Boris Yeltsin, a member of parliament, to be their new president. In a desperate action to keep the Soviet Union in Communist Party hands, the conservative State Committee detained Gorbachev and ordered the military to attack the parliament. This August Coup (August 19-21, 1991) failed when soldiers stepped out of their tanks and refused to fight for the Communist conspirators.

13. **B**. The Soviet Union dissolved into the CIS, or Commonwealth of Independent States. Former republics, such as Ukraine, would become an independent state. Also, Russia would once again become a country.

14. **A**. In 1990, East and West Germany came together in a process called reunification. The Berlin Wall came down a year earlier.

15. **C**. With the economy weakening, Poland, with help from Lech Walesa and his labor union Solidarity, was able to get free elections in 1989. Soon after, Poland was free from communist rule.

16. **A**. Yugoslavia experienced bloody conflict as it broke apart. With different ethnic groups in the area, there was a struggle for territory. In Bosnia-Herzegovina, *ethnic cleansing*, or the violent elimination of a group from an area, occurred as Serbian forces attempted to remove Muslim influences from Bosnia. Ethnic cleansing involved executions and other human rights violations.

17. **A**. The Korean War ended in 1953 leaving an estimated death toll in the millions. In the aftermath, massive American aid poured into South Korea for decades. The 38th parallel is still the dividing line in Korea today, as North and South are buffered by a demilitarized zone (DMZ).

18. **A**. The Domino Theory was a belief in the United States that if one nation in Asia fell to communism, then the neighboring nations would also fall...like dominos. It was important to stop that first country from becoming communist.

19. **D**. In 1954, the French saw the city of Dien Bien Phu fall to the communists and their leader Ho Chi Minh. Minh used nationalism as

a unifying force to drive out the French, and spread communism.

20. **A**. The United States escalated their forces in Vietnam with the Gulf of Tonkin Resolution of 1964. The North Vietnamese attacked South Vietnam in the 1968 Tet Offensive. In 1973, a ceasefire and peace was announced. Shortly after American troops left the region, Vietnam became communist. Saigon became Ho Chi Minh City.

21. **B**. When the United States pulled out of Vietnam, the country turned communist. Communism spread to neighboring Cambodia. In 1975 a group called the Khmer Rouge set up a government under their leader Pol Pot. He hoped to create a collectivized agricultural state. Under Pol Pot's reign (1975-1979), genocide occurred, as an estimated 2 million Cambodians were killed through forced labor, or execution. The sites of the atrocities are commonly referred to as the Killing Fields.

22. **A**. Kennedy is speaking of the weakness of appeasement, or giving into the aggressor's demands. Britain and France permitted Hitler to expand and violate the Treaty of Versailles with hopes that it would lead to peace.

23. **D**. When US intelligence learned of the missiles, Kennedy took it as a threat of war. His solution was to: 1. Blockade (quarantine) Cuba by surrounding it with US naval ships. The goal was to prevent the delivery of Soviet weapons. 2. Threaten force if Khrushchev did not remove the missiles. The missiles were removed.

# China and India After 1900

1. Sun Yixian's Three Principles of the Chinese people looked to
   A) appeal to peasants seeking a socialist alternative to capitalism
   B) support the leadership of the Qing emperor
   C) increase allegiance to Japan as an ally
   D) ensure the rights of Chinese citizens

2. All of the following were reasons why the Chinese people found communism appealing EXCEPT:
   A) Communists supported land reform and equality to peasants
   B) Communism was proven strong in the Soviet Union
   C) There was a desire to rid the country of Japanese interests
   D) Jiang Jieshi's propaganda campaign led to popular support for communism

3. Nationalists and Communists united during the Chinese Civil War when
   A) Joseph Stalin aligned with the Axis Powers
   B) Japan invaded Manchuria
   C) Pearl Harbor was attacked
   D) the Chinese emperor refused to abdicate the throne

4. Which of the following was NOT true of Mao Zedong's Long March?
   A) Mao Zedong avoided capture
   B) Communist supporters were recruited during the march
   C) It was roughly 6,000 miles in length
   D) It ended with Mao's victory in Beijing's Tiananmen Square

5. Mao's Great Leap Forward resulted in
   A) successful modernization of China's industry
   B) the spread of communes throughout China
   C) strong harvests and surplus crops
   D) well-crafted goods to be exported to the United States

6. The Cultural Revolution of Mao Zedong led to
   A) massive industrialization near the Yangtze River
   B) a strong communist grip over the people
   C) the promotion of intellectuals within government
   D) the spread of Enlightenment ideas

7. After the Tiananmen Square Massacre, China experienced

A) many more protests and demonstrations against communism
B) economic and political punishments from the United Nations
C) a reduction in resistance against the government
D) a decrease in industrialization

8. Which program was most responsible for the emergence of China as a world economic power in the twenty-first century?

A) Great Leap Forward
B) Four Modernizations
C) Cultural Revolution
D) Three Principles

9. Which area of China has often accused the Chinese government of human rights violations?

A) Tibet
B) Xi'an
C) Chongqing
D) Shanghai

10. The Three Gorges Dam is considered a major economic success for China because it

A) makes the Yangtze River more navigable
B) has created valuable sources of energy
C) establishes a natural border between China and India
D) cuts in half the duration of travel between Beijing and Xi'an

11. The actions of Indian protesters at Amritsar resulted in

A) a human rights violation
B) repeal of the Rowlatt Act
C) more rights for sepoy soldiers
D) the partition of India

12. Which of the following is an example of civil disobedience?

A) Parliament passing a law which is enforced on only certain citizens
B) Violent revolutionary activity
C) Refusing to obey a law seen as unjust
D) Segregation of the races

13. Mohandas K. Gandhi and his supporters protested the British Raj in all of the following ways EXCEPT:

A) Boycotts of British goods
B) Marching for salt
C) Refusals to pay taxes
D) Denial of support for World War I

14. Which of the following was true of the partition of India?

A) Britain continued to control Pakistan for decades
B) Muhammad Ali Jinnah led a Hindu state
C) Pakistan would be greatly influenced by Islam
D) Mohandas K. Gandhi refused to negotiate with Muslim officials

15. Because of a split in culture and political decision making, East Pakistan became

A) Nepal
B) Myanmar
C) Sri Lanka
D) Bangladesh

16. Why has the caste system been an obstacle for democracy in India?

A) traditional values can hinder equal rights
B) political opportunity is only an option for the highest caste
C) the election process conflicts with traditional culture
D) women have not been allowed to take part in the political process

17. Critics of modern industrialization in both China and India are MOST concerned with
   A) overpopulation
   B) pollution
   C) nuclear proliferation
   D) deforestation

18. The first woman elected to lead a Muslim state was
   A) Indira Gandhi
   B) Benazir Bhutto
   C) Aung San Suu Kyi
   D) Golda Meir

19. The Tamil Tigers fought for a homeland in
   A) the Philippines
   B) Jakarta
   C) Sri Lanka
   D) Pakistan

Question 20 is based on the photos of modern China below.

20. Which of the following can best be concluded by the above pictures?
   A) Rapid industrialization can have negative impacts on traditional society
   B) Pollution has been a major consequence of industrialization
   C) Deng Xiaoping's Four Modernizations were not successful
   D) Most structures in China have been built on waterways

## Answers and Explanations

1. **D**. Dr. Sun Yixian of the Kuomintang (political party known as the Nationalist Party) helped overthrow the Qing emperor. Yixian promised Three Principles of the Chinese people. They were: 1. Nationalism/People's Rule - This meant to bring unity and pride to the Chinese people who had been imperialized by foreign nations for almost a century. 2. Democracy - A goal of creating a government that met the needs of the people and ensured rights. 3. People's Livelihood - Making sure that everyone had a comfortable standard of living.

2. **D**. Jiang Jieshi took over China when Sun Yixian died, and ruled as a dictator. He was anti-communist and ordered the execution of many communist supporters.

3. **B**. The Japanese invaded Manchuria (northern China) in 1931, thereby starting World War II in Asia. They were attracted to the area because of an abundance of raw materials such as coal and iron. By the late 1930s, they had a stronghold in China. This forced Jiang Jieshi and Mao Zedong to agree to a ceasefire, thereby becoming reluctant allies against Japan.

4. **D**. It seemed that by 1934 the Communists were all but defeated. However, Mao Zedong went on a 6,000 mile trek known as the Long March. As he paraded around the country, he avoided capture and gathered supporters. The longer the war went on, the better it was for Mao. However, Mao wouldn't claim victory in Beijing's Tiananmen Square until 1949…long after the march.

5. **B**. The Great Leap Forward was Mao's plan to develop agriculture and industry. People were forced to live with other families on large plots of land called communes. Here, they collectively worked together. Citizens were encouraged to create furnaces in their backyards to make steel materials. Despite the increase in production, the Great Leap Forward was mostly a failure because bad weather and depleted agricultural workforces led to poor harvests and famines that killed millions. Furthermore, there was an overproduction of shoddy finished goods.

6. **B**. In the Cultural Revolution, Mao's government unleashed a massive censorship campaign that targeted intellectuals or any who dissented with the rule of the Communist Party. Chinese citizens were instructed to carry a Little Red Book entitled *Quotations from Chairman Mao*, which contained his famous speeches and thoughts.

7. **C**. In 1989, students protested communist rule and peacefully campaigned for democracy in Beijing's Tiananmen Square. Deng Xiaoping's soldiers opened fire, killing many protesters. Although the massacre was condemned by nations around the world, demonstrations in China were quickly silenced. Estimates of the dead and wounded exceed 2,000.

8. **B**. Today, China is one of the leading industrial powers in the world. However until about 1980, it lagged behind most other nations. Deng Xiaoping helped get the ball rolling on massive industrialization with a program called the Four Modernizations. Inheriting this policy from a decade before, he set new goals for agriculture, industry, and technology. Small businesses were permitted to operate, and with their profits, people began to purchase consumer goods.

9. **A.** Once an independent country, Tibet is a region in western China. The People's Republic of China took over the area in the early 1950s, but promised autonomy to the Tibetans and their religious leader, the Dalai Lama. However, Tibet never gained self-rule. Through the years, several uprisings have led to deportations. The Tibetans cite human rights violations. The Chinese government denies these claims. Despite international pressure, Tibet remains part of China.

10. **B.** China continues to grow at an incredible rate. Huge building projects, such as the Three Gorges Dam (mostly operational by 2008) on the Yangtze River, surpassed other similar worldwide constructions. The dam is responsible for harnessing massive amounts of electrical power.

11. **A.** When a group of Hindus and Muslims assembled in the city of Amritsar to give political speeches (thereby violating the Rowlatt Act which forbid such speech), British officer Reginald Dyer ordered his troops to fire. Hundreds were killed, and almost 1,500 were wounded. The massacre led to immense anti-British sentiment amongst the Indian people.

12. **C.** Mohandas K. Gandhi led a push for Indian independence from the British crown. His methods and education combined both Western and Eastern thought. Gandhi preached civil disobedience (disobeying laws seen as unjust) and passive resistance (peaceful protest).

13. **D.** Resistance was achieved through powerful boycotts of British finished goods (specifically spun goods), refusal to pay taxes, a march for salt, and a lack of government participation. Choice D is correct because sepoys, or British soldiers of Indian descent, supported World War I activity.

14. **C.** India's fight for independence from Britain gave way to an internal struggle among religions. When Britain withdrew from India in 1947, the country was divided (partitioned) into the independent nations of India, which was mostly comprised of Hindus, and Pakistan, which was mostly populated by Muslims.

15. **D.** Originally, partition led to both West Pakistan and East Pakistan. Many miles apart, these two nations had differences of opinion. Bangladesh emerged in the East.

16. **A.** Because the social hierarchy of the caste system has been in place for thousands of years, democracy faces certain challenges in India.

17. **B.** With the massive industrial output of this populated area of the world, nations have criticized the amount of pollution that has resulted from intense industrialization.

18. **B.** In Pakistan, Benazir Bhutto became the first woman ever elected to lead a Muslim state. After facing corruption charges, she exiled herself in 1998. She returned in 2007, and was assassinated as she campaigned for public office.

19. **C**. A militant separatist group from Southern India known as the Tamil Tigers fought for a homeland in Buddhist Sri Lanka. From 1983-2009 there was a civil war. The Tamil Tigers engaged in guerilla military and terror activities. They never gained a homeland in Sri Lanka.

20. **A**. The picture on the left shows traditional architecture being overshadowed by a modern structure on the Yangtze River in China. The picture on the right shows a huge traffic jam in the city of Wuhan. For Choice B, although pollution is a concern, the pictures do not show that evidence.

# Post-World War II Middle East, Africa, and the Modern World

1. Which of the following was an example of Zionism?
   A) North American Free Trade Agreement
   B) Kyoto Protocol
   C) Convention at Kanagawa
   D) Balfour Declaration

2. Who of the following was leader of the Palestine Liberation Organization?
   A) Gamal Abdel Nasser
   B) Ayatollah Khomeini
   C) Saddam Hussein
   D) Yasser Arafat

3. The government set up by Ayatollah Khomeini after the Iranian Revolution looked to
   A) embrace communism
   B) establish Islamic law
   C) increase imports of Western capital goods
   D) restore the Shah to power

4. Which of the following was NOT a conflict between Israel and the Arab World between 1948-1973?
   A) Yom Kippur War
   B) Boer Wars
   C) Six-Day War
   D) Suez Crisis

5. OPEC is most influential because they
   A) can control the supply of oil to much of the world
   B) have a monopoly of the world's oil
   C) can force countries to stop producing fossil fuels
   D) decide which forms of renewable energy can be produced

6. In 2006, which group won political power in Gaza?
   A) Taliban
   B) Hezbollah
   C) Hamas
   D) al-Qaeda

7. Apartheid in South Africa led to
   A) separation of the races
   B) genocide of certain religious sects
   C) liberation of women
   D) removal of Dutch and English influences

8. Which of the following was true of apartheid?
   A) It was started by the French in South Africa in 1948
   B) Nelson Mandela of the African National Congress was imprisoned in Britain
   C) F.W. de Klerk legislated for the beginning of apartheid
   D) Foreign nations leveled sanctions and trade embargoes to help end apartheid

9. Jomo Kenyatta and Kwame Nkrumah were both associated with
    A) bringing an end to apartheid
    B) African independence movements
    C) spreading Enlightenment ideas to South Africa
    D) opening up trade and westernization in central Africa

10. Which is true of the Rwandan Genocide of 1994?
    A) Hutus were the minority of the population
    B) Tutsis were the targets of the majority of the violence
    C) NATO restored order to the region
    D) The conflict spread to Darfur

11. Which of the following South American nations has been industrializing at the quickest rate in the twenty-first century?
    A) Brazil
    B) Colombia
    C) Peru
    D) Uruguay

12. The Green Revolution was responsible for
    A) spreading nuclear energy around the globe
    B) eliminating fossil fuel pollutants
    C) banning chemical pesticides
    D) increasing the amount of food in the world

13. The European Union is best described as a
    A) fragmented union of former Warsaw Pact nations
    B) United Nations agency
    C) federation that has its headquarters in Berlin
    D) political association of various European countries

14. All of the following exhibit examples of global interdependence EXCEPT:
    A) Stock markets in the United States affecting prices in Japan
    B) Nations coming together to donate money to earthquake ravaged areas
    C) More food being harvested in Canada after a mild summer
    D) The United States receiving help from other countries in the War on Terror

## Answers and Explanations

1. **D.** Led by Theodor Herzl, Zionism was a movement in the late nineteenth century to find a permanent homeland for Jews in the Holy Land of the Middle East. In 1917, a letter (known as the Balfour Declaration) written by British Foreign Secretary Arthur James Balfour called for the formation of a Jewish state within Palestine of the Middle East. The Jewish state of Israel was created after World War II.

2. **D.** In the 1970s, the PLO (Palestine Liberation Organization) was led by Yasser Arafat. Arafat hoped to get self-determination for a Palestinian State. Much violence occurred in the area. In 1993 President Bill Clinton attempted to bring peace between Arafat and Israeli Prime Minister Yitzhak Rabin. Israel agreed to withdraw some troops and permit Palestinians to self-govern the territories of the Gaza Strip and West Bank.

3. **B.** In 1978, anti-Western riots spread throughout Iran. To control order, martial law (emergency military rule) was established by Western ally Mohammad Reza Pahlavi - the Shah of Iran. Still, opposition mounted. As his popularity decreased, the Shah fled Iran and Ayatollah Khomeini took power in 1979. Khomeini supported an Islamic state, not a westernized one.

4. **B.** The Boer Wars occurred in South Africa many decades earlier. The other three were conflicts between Israel and the Arab world.

5. **A.** The Organization of the Petroleum Exporting Countries is a very influential union of the world's largest oil producing nations such as Iran, Saudi Arabia, and Venezuela. They control the production of much of the globe's crude oil supply. Therefore, they have great influence on the worldwide prices of oil and gasoline products.

6. **C.** In 2006, Hamas won elections in Gaza. The Taliban reigned in Afghanistan, and Hezbollah in Lebanon. The terrorist organization al-Qaeda spread through the Middle East in the late twentieth and early twenty-first centuries.

7. **A.** Given self-rule from Great Britain, the Republic of South Africa's white National Party members and Afrikaners (Dutch descendants) discriminated against black Africans. Apartheid (notice the word apart) was a separation of the majority black population from the minority white race in South Africa. The entire country was legally segregated for nearly 50 years, from 1948-1994.

8. **D.** Countries leveled sanctions (economic punishments) and trade embargos on South Africa. In 1990 F.W. de Klerk, the new President of South Africa, released Mandela. Soon after, apartheid ended. When all people were allowed to vote in 1994, the African National Congress gained control of the Parliament and Mandela became President. In 1996, a new democratic constitution was adopted for the Republic of South Africa.

9. **B.** Both were involved with independence movements. Kwame Nkrumah helped the British Gold Coast become an independent Ghana in 1957. Jomo Kenyatta was the first president of Kenya after it received independence from Britain in 1963.

10. **B.** Two rival ethnic groups exist in Rwanda…Hutus (the majority) and Tutsis. For centuries, there has been conflict. In reaction to the death of the Hutu president, genocide occurred. For about 100 days an estimated 800,000 Tutsis were killed, mostly by Hutus. Many Tutsis fled the country until the Rwandan Patriotic Front (RPF) restored order.

11. **A.** Developing nations are those who are slowly becoming industrialized. Developed nations have established themselves as having manufacturing centers and more advanced economies. The fastest industrializing nations since 2000 have been Asian countries like China and India, and Latin American ones such as Brazil. Brazil won rights to host the Summer Olympics in 2016.

12. **D.** New farming techniques, chemical pesticides, and fertilizers increased crop yields in the twentieth century. More food for consumption meant less world hunger. Think: Lettuce is green, and so was this revolution.

13. **D.** The Maastricht Treaty of 1992 established the European Union a year later. The EU is a political union between certain European Nations. The EU allows people to travel freely through member nations, creates common legislation, and operates on the currency of the Euro.

14. **C.** In recent years, nations have become dependent on each other. They also can have their livelihood affected by events thousands of miles away. In 2008, when the stock market took a dive in the United States, markets around the world were affected. When the 2004 tsunami hit Indonesia, or the 2010 earthquake devastated Haiti, the rest of the world helped out. With information readily available on television and the internet, the entire world has become a network of dependent nations. Choice C does not show that type of contact.

# 135 More Practice Questions

1.  • Achievements in algebra
    • People observe religious ceremonies in Mecca
    • Golden Age included advances in calligraphy

The above statements speak of facts regarding which region?
A) China
B) The Middle East
C) India
D) Latin America

2. Which of the following religions follows the Eightfold Path?
A) Hinduism
B) Buddhism
C) Shintoism
D) Islam

3. Which of the following religions was founded most recently?
A) Judaism
B) Christianity
C) Hinduism
D) Islam

4. One similarity between the Sumerians and the Egyptians was
A) the use of a writing system
B) utilization of the Nile River
C) adherence to Hammurabi's Code
D) adoption of monotheism

5. Which of the following leaders destroyed the first Holy Temple of Jerusalem?
A) Alexander the Great
B) Asoka
C) Nebuchadnezzar II
D) Julius Caesar

6. Which idea is central to Zoroastrianism?
A) Forces of good and evil battle for the soul
B) Only a life of devout prayer will lead to salvation
C) The worshipping of Incan deities is crucial
D) Actions cannot change one's destiny

7. Which was true of Harappa and Mohenjo-Daro?
A) Both had advanced plumbing networks
B) They were fortified cities along the Yangtze River
C) Monotheism flourished in both cities
D) There were heavy influences of Hellenistic culture within their walls

8   • Founded by Chandragupta
    • Asoka was a strong leader
    • Empire predated the Gupta

The above facts are true of which empire?
A) Tang
B) Mughal
C) Mauryan
D) Ming

9. Monsoons are important to India because
A) they help isolate the land from neighboring China
B) predictable storms are vital for agriculture
C) they are necessary to prevent beach erosion
D) trade routes depend on them for interaction

Questions 10-12 are based on the following speakers.

**Speaker 1**: Filial piety is important, as one must respect their elders. Furthermore, one must respect the major relationships between people.
**Speaker 2**: People must follow "the way" and accept the forces of nature.
**Speaker 3**: A strong government must maintain order through whatever means necessary.
**Speaker 4**: Everything in life is suffering. This suffering is caused by selfish desires for fleeting pleasure.

10. Who of the following would most likely agree with Speaker 3?
A) Confucius
B) Laozi
C) Shi Huangdi
D) Muhammad

11. Which philosophy would be incorporated into the Han Dynasty?
A) Speaker 1
B) Speaker 2
C) Speaker 3
D) Speaker 4

12. Which speaker reflects the ideas of Siddhartha Gautama?
A) Speaker 1
B) Speaker 2
C) Speaker 3
D) Speaker 4

13. Zheng He was influential in
A) introducing Islam to Africa
B) bringing peace within the Roman Empire
C) ending the reign of the Han Dynasty
D) connecting the cultures of the Eastern Hemisphere

Questions 14-16 are based on the map below.

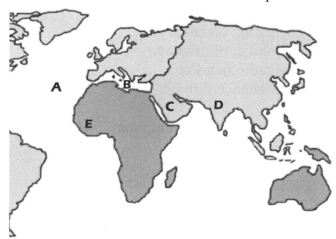

14. Which region was vital for the gold-salt trade?
A) A
B) B
C) C
D) D
E) E

15. Which important waterway is B referring to?
A) Aegean Sea
B) Adriatic Sea
C) Mediterranean Sea
D) Baltic Sea

16. In which region was the Qur'an (Koran) first introduced as holy scripture?
A) A
B) B
C) C
D) D
E) E

17. Which of the following leaders performed the hajj?
   A) Alexander the Great
   B) Mansa Musa
   C) King Darius
   D) Nebuchadnezzar II

18. The Neolithic Revolution led to a decrease in
   A) irrigation techniques
   B) animal domestication
   C) nomadic families
   D) subsistence farmers

19. A physical map would most likely be used when highlighting the
   A) capitals of countries and provinces
   B) changing populations of towns
   C) species present in an area
   D) presence of mountains and vegetation

20. Which mountain range isolated southern China from northern India?
   A) Andes
   B) Urals
   C) Himalayas
   D) Caucasus

Question 21 is based on the photo below.

21. The geography in the above picture is most useful for
   A) aiding in slash-and-burn farming
   B) distributing nutrients during rainstorms
   C) helping with crop rotation
   D) providing subsistence farming for nuclear families.

22. How did the first inhabitants of the New World arrive in the Western Hemisphere?
   A) Long sea voyages from China brought them to the west coast of America
   B) A land-bridge linked Asia to North America
   C) They arrived when Europe was still connected to eastern Canada
   D) Egyptian trade vessels brought cultures into Mesoamerica

23. Tenochtitlan and Teotihuacan were both
   A) important trading destinations in the gold-salt exchange
   B) cultural centers for the Aztec Empire
   C) Incan religious temples in Peru
   D) places conquered by the Olmec civilization before European colonization

24. Mongol trade routes connected cultures in all of the following regions EXCEPT:
   A) Mali
   B) Russia
   C) Middle East
   D) India

Question 25 is based on the photo below.

25. The above pyramid was an architectural achievement of the
    A) Egyptians
    B) Mayans
    C) Mughals
    D) Guptas

26. Which invention is attributed to the Song Dynasty?
    A) Block type
    B) The astrolabe
    C) Paper money
    D) Written laws

27. The Gupta Empire was known for
    A) expanding their territory into Northern China
    B) cultural interactions with travelers from South America
    C) utilizing the concept of zero in complex mathematics
    D) applying Greek thought to Hindu religious ideas

28. The Mayan and Abbasid Empires both shared
    A) an impressive knowledge of astronomy
    B) a devout faith in one God
    C) extensive use of terrace farming
    D) trade networks which reached Rome

29. China's Mandate of Heaven, the European concept of divine right, and Egypt's theocracy all believed in
    A) a representative democracy where people were elected to serve
    B) totalitarian governments where the state dictated religious adherence
    C) support of an intellectual elite to lead government
    D) a connection between the ruler on Earth to the heavens above

30. Marco Polo and Ibn Battuta were similar in that both
    A) were honored in the court of Kublai Khan
    B) brought trade to the Aztec Empire
    C) spread Christianity to new cultures in Asia
    D) established cultural connections across the Eastern Hemisphere

31. • Questioned the world around him
    • Convicted of corrupting the youth of Athens
    • Early pioneer of Western philosophy

The above statements explain the life of
    A) Socrates
    B) Plato
    C) Aristotle
    D) Alexander the Great

32. The ideas of Hippocrates had the greatest influence on
   A) literature
   B) math
   C) medicine
   D) athletics

33. Which of the following is true regarding the Persian and Peloponnesian Wars?
   A) The Peloponnesian War resulted in a golden age for Athens
   B) Athens and Sparta were allies in defeating invaders in the Persian Wars
   C) The Persian Wars resulted in the defeat of Sparta, and the significant loss of Greek land to the Persian Empire
   D) Alexander the Great was triumphant in the Persian Wars, but not the Peloponnesian War

34. A government ruled by an aristocracy is controlled by
   A) one king
   B) two monarchs
   C) a wealthy class of nobles
   D) an elected Senate

35. Patricians in the Roman Republic were
   A) commoners who lacked education
   B) dictators who could govern in times of war
   C) powerful landowners
   D) educated peasants with political power

36. Pax Romana and Pax Mongolica were similar in that both
   A) were times of peace which led to cultural and economic stability
   B) led to the spread of Christianity throughout each empire
   C) created division between emperors and legislatures
   D) led to isolation and an end to trading with other civilizations

37. Why are Greece and Rome considered important contributors to Western civilization?
   A) Both preserved Christian thought before spreading it to the rest of the world
   B) The farming techniques of Greece and Rome revolutionized agriculture around the globe
   C) Many cultural ideas of the region spread to Europe centuries later
   D) The direct democracy of Greece was continued in Rome, and later used all over Europe

38. Which religion was adopted by much of the Byzantine Empire in 1054 CE?
   A) Roman Catholicism
   B) Eastern Orthodox
   C) Islam
   D) Judaism

Question 39 is based on the selection below.

"Roman citizens are bound together in lawful matrimony when they are united according to law…they must first obtain the consent of their parents, in whose power they are. For both natural reason and the law require this consent; so much so, indeed, that it ought to precede the marriage."

- Justinian's Code, c530CE

39. The purpose of the above law was to
   A) prevent people from getting married without family approval
   B) permit women to marry anybody within or outside the Roman Empire
   C) prevent marriages from being performed between people of different cultural backgrounds
   D) permit the Emperor to discredit marriages that were seen as immoral

40. In Medieval feudal culture, which was true of serfdom?

A) Serfs would often marry into the family of vassals

B) Serfdom was abolished through stipulations in the Magna Carta

C) Serfs could not freely travel

D) Serfs were the only people who worked on the manor

41. Which of the following groups invaded England from the region of Scandinavia?

A) Vikings

B) Magyars

C) Moors

D) Huns

42. The Medieval knight and the feudal samurai warrior of Japan both

A) exclusively used gunpowder as a means of defending castles

B) fought on the same side during the Crusades

C) helped spread Christianity throughout their respective regions

D) adhered to a strict code of ethics to honor those around them

43. Burghers were Medieval people who were

A) merchants or artisans

B) vassals who served under a knight

C) kings of small regions of Europe

D) apprentices first learning a skill

44. Which of the following was a punishment used by the Catholic Church?

A) Simony

B) Excommunication

C) Lay investiture

D) Indulgence

45. Pope Urban II was most associated with the

A) Great Schism

B) Spanish Inquisition

C) Crusades

D) Protestant Reformation

46. How do most historians believe the bubonic plague was brought to Europe?

A) The disease was exchanged through trade on the Silk Roads

B) It was introduced during the First Crusade

C) Invaders who sacked Rome in the fifth century spread it

D) Trading vessels from Asia brought the disease to Italy

47. Why was the Renaissance considered to be a "rebirth"?

A) Religion proved to be weak during the Middle Ages, and the Renaissance revived it

B) Greco-Roman culture, which was somewhat dormant during the Medieval period, thrived during the Renaissance

C) The Renaissance was the first time in world history where cultures could connect with each other on an educational basis

D) Newly discovered culture from the ancient Egyptians and Babylonians fostered new thought

48. "Still, a prince should make himself feared in such a way that if he does not gain love, he at any rate avoids hatred; for fear and the absence of hatred may well go together." - 1513

The above words can be attributed to which author?

A) Niccolò Machiavelli

B) Thomas More

C) Thomas Aquinas

D) Dante Alighieri

49. The Renaissance and the Golden Age of Islam were both movements that
   A) spread Islam throughout the Eastern Hemisphere
   B) created new thought that is still influential today
   C) brought an end to the Crusades
   D) expanded knowledge without the use of printing technology

50. Compared to Medieval art, Renaissance art was
   A) less colorful
   B) out of proportion
   C) more realistic
   D) two-dimensional

51. All of the following were results of the Protestant Reformation EXCEPT:
   A) An increase in the number of religious sects in Europe
   B) Violent religious conflicts in Western Europe
   C) A reformation within the Roman Catholic Church
   D) The strengthening of Roman Catholicism in England

52. Which of the following splits in the Church was most affected by the invention of the printing press?
   A) East-West schism of 1054
   B) The Great Schism
   C) Protestant Reformation
   D) Counter-Reformation

53.    • People live as hunters and gatherers
       • Bantu languages expand throughout the region
       • Many people practice animism

The above observations reflect life in ancient
   A) Egypt
   B) Central Africa
   C) Native America
   D) Mesopotamia

54. An extended patrilineal family would be one that lives
   A) in a small unit but traces ancestry through the father
   B) with many relatives and traces ancestry through the mother
   C) in a small unit but traces ancestry through the mother
   D) with many relatives and traces ancestry through the father

55. The Songhai city of Timbuktu was important because it
   A) was the birthplace of Islamic thought
   B) became an important trading center in the region
   C) was home to much of western Africa's gold
   D) bordered the Mediterranean Sea, and led to contact with Europe

56. Islamic Empires were strong in all of the following regions EXCEPT:
   A) Northern Africa
   B) Southern Spain
   C) Western Asia
   D) Southern France

57. Which of the following best exemplifies cultural diffusion?

A) Absolute monarchy
B) The Columbian Exchange
C) Terrace farming
D) Hammurabi's Code

58. All of the following were true of Peter the Great EXCEPT:

A) He adapted western culture within his Empire
B) He expanded rights to women in Russia
C) He embraced and implemented the ideas of Voltaire
D) He used serf labor to build a new city on the Neva River

59. The Edict of Nantes and the Edict of Milan were important in

A) expanding religious toleration
B) providing favorable trading rights
C) establishing a policy of freedom of the seas
D) securing overseas territories for the nations of Europe

60. The Magna Carta (1215), Habeas Corpus Act (1679), and English Bill of Rights (1689) were ALL influential in

A) decreasing the power of Parliament over the English people
B) expanding rights against cruel and unusual punishment
C) narrowing the gap between the rich and the poor
D) limiting the power of the absolute monarch

61. Which strong Central European Hapsburg ruler was a devout Catholic, but not tolerant of other religious sects?

A) Catherine the Great
B) Elizabeth Tudor
C) Maria Theresa
D) Marie Antoinette

62.
• Voiced, "I am the state."
• Nicknamed the Sun King
• Constructed lavish architecture

The above statements reflect facts concerning which European monarch?

A) Charles I
B) Louis XIV
C) Charles II
D) Louis XVI

63. Which of the following monarchs would be considered an "enlightened despot"?

A) Louis XIV
B) James II
C) Frederick the Great
D) Ivan the Terrible

64. Socrates and Galileo Galilei were similar in that both

A) made landmark astrological observations
B) were labeled as heretics by the Catholic Church
C) were forced to stop preaching their knowledge
D) suffered a fate of execution

65. Mohandas K. Gandhi and Jean-Jacques Rousseau both voiced strongly that

A) India should be free from British control

B) people should resist laws that were seen as unjust

C) separation of powers was the solution for tyrannical government

D) freedom of speech should be absolute for the highest classes only

66. Mary Wollstonecraft was known for expressing that

A) women should have equal opportunities in education

B) bicameral legislatures were necessary to ensure democratic reforms

C) Louis XIV was an inefficient leader

D) the planets of the solar system revolve around the sun

67. Which of the following was true of the bourgeoisie in eighteenth century France?

A) Most of them were strong supporters of the Old Regime

B) Many tended to be well-educated with Enlightenment thought

C) Most resisted capitalism and trade in favor of socialism

D) They were more numerous than the peasantry

68. A late eighteenth century consequence of the French Revolution was

A) an end to monarchy in Europe

B) a military coup d'état

C) a lengthy peace and economic prosperity

D) the isolation of France

69. One similarity between Napoleon Bonaparte and Adolf Hitler was that both

A) were born in the country that they led

B) could not successfully control Britain or Russia

C) became Allies with Japan

D) were not successful in taking over France

70. Which is true of the *Declaration of the Rights of Man and of the Citizen*?

A) It eliminated the need for a strong legislature

B) It set a precedent for the American Declaration of Independence

C) It influenced independence movements far away from France

D) It supported the idea of an absolute monarchy

71. Which was a major difference between the Haitian and Venezuelan independence movements?

A) Only Haiti was inspired by Enlightenment thought

B) Haiti's movement was led by Simón Bolívar while Venezuela's was not

C) Haiti revolted against the Spanish while Venezuela did so against the French

D) Only the movement in Haiti was an uprising of slaves

72. The unifications of Italy and Germany were similar in that they both

A) were inspired by the writings of Karl Marx

B) used peaceful diplomacy instead of force

C) desired to gain the territories of Alsace and Lorraine

D) exhibited strong nationalistic sentiment among the people

Questions 73-76 are based on the the following speakers from the eighteenth and nineteenth centuries.

**Speaker 1**: "The great questions of the day will not be settled by means of speeches and majority decisions but by iron and blood."

**Speaker 2**: "One general law, leading to the advancement of all organic beings, namely, multiply, vary, let the strongest live and the weakest die."

**Speaker 3**: "Take up the White Man's burden—The savage wars of peace—Fill full the mouth of Famine, And bid the sickness cease…"

**Speaker 4**: "It is not from the benevolence of the butcher, the brewer, or the baker, that we expect our dinner, but from their regard to their own self-interest."

73. Which of the above speakers is commentating about imperialistic endeavors?
    A) Speaker 1
    B) Speaker 2
    C) Speaker 3
    D) Speaker 4

74. Speaker 1 reflects the ideas of
    A) Camillo di Cavour
    B) Giuseppe Garibaldi
    C) Kaiser Wilhelm II
    D) Otto von Bismarck

75. Who of the following objected to some of the research performed by Speaker 2?
    A) Members of the clergy
    B) Absolute monarchs
    C) Enlightenment thinkers
    D) Successful entrepreneurs

76. Speaker 4 would most likely favor
    A) the sharing of the factors of production
    B) free-enterprise and capitalism
    C) extensive government regulation of businesses
    D) a traditional economy based on barter

Questions 77-78 are based on the selection below.

"The increasing improvement of machinery, ever more rapidly developing, makes their livelihood more and more precarious; the collisions between individual workmen and individual bourgeois take more and more the character of collisions between two classes. Thereupon, the workers begin to form combinations (trade unions) against the bourgeois; they club together in order to keep up the rate of wages; they found permanent associations in order to make provision beforehand for these occasional revolts. Here and there, the contest breaks out into riots."

– Karl Marx and Friedrich Engels,
*The Communist Manifesto*, 1848

77. What opinion do the above authors have concerning the Industrial Revolution?
    A) The Industrial Revolution has created much class struggle
    B) New inventions have had a positive influence on the expansion of industry
    C) Trade unions will always succeed in negotiations
    D) Wages must be kept low to increase the profits of the employers of industry

78. Which Asian country would be LEAST affected by the above authors in the twentieth century?

A) Japan
B) China
C) Cambodia
D) Vietnam

79. Which of the following is true of the Industrial Revolution?

A) It began in Eastern Europe and then spread west
B) The transformations in the economy led to increased urbanization
C) Pollution resulting from the Industrial Revolution didn't become a problem until the twentieth century
D) Most workers received high wages and favorable working conditions

80. The Dreyfus Affair in France and the pogroms in Russia were both examples of

A) anti-Semitism
B) unification movements
C) European imperialism
D) communist uprisings

81. The Boer Wars, Opium Wars and Boxer Rebellion all

A) took place in Asia
B) were measures to resist imperialism
C) resulted in a weakening of the British Empire
D) were inspired by the French Revolution

82. Which of the following was a goal of imperialism in the nineteenth century?

A) Transporting a majority of the imperialist nation's population to foreign lands
B) Converting Europeans to the religions of the imperialized
C) Depleting the raw materials of Europe and bringing them to foreign countries
D) Introducing the culture of Europe to far-off lands

Questions 83-85 are based on the map below.

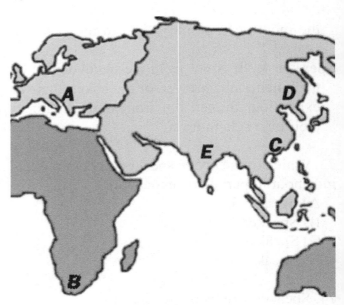

83. Which of the above places was the site of the spark that triggered World War I?

A) A
B) B
C) C
D) D
E) E

84. Which area was most affected by the Treaty of Nanjing, which ended the first Opium War?
   A) A
   B) B
   C) C
   D) D
   E) E

85. Which of the following is true of D on the map?
   A) It would become a target for Japan to secure raw materials
   B) It was considered the "jewel of the crown" of the British Empire
   C) It was the location of Germany's surrender during World War I
   D) It was the site of most of Mao Zedong's Long March

86. Which empire was quickly losing power just before the outbreak of World War I?
   A) Holy Roman Empire
   B) Ottoman Empire
   C) Mughal Empire
   D) Gupta Empire

87. Fighting in World War I ended on November 11, 1918 when
   A) Woodrow Wilson delivered his Fourteen Points speech
   B) Kaiser Wilhelm agreed to an armistice
   C) The Treaty of Versailles was signed
   D) The Zimmermann Telegram was intercepted

Question 88 is based on the selection below.

"XIV. A general association of nations must be formed under specific covenants for the purpose of affording mutual guarantees of political independence and territorial integrity to great and small states alike."
   – Woodrow Wilson, January 8, 1918

88. The above idea would become a reality with the
   A) formation of the League of Nations
   B) signing of the Atlantic Charter
   C) chartering of the United Nations
   D) signing of the Kellogg-Briand Pact

89. What territory did Russia lose after World War I?
   A) Yugoslavia
   B) Estonia
   C) Czechoslovakia
   D) Afghanistan

90. All of the following were seen as weaknesses of Czar Nicholas II EXCEPT:
   A) The use of force on Bloody Sunday
   B) Loss to Japan in the Russo-Japanese War
   C) Collectivization of land and farms of the wealthy
   D) High rate of casualties during World War I

91. Who would become leader of the Provisional Government of Russia after the March Revolution of 1917?
   A) Vladimir Lenin
   B) Alexander Kerensky
   C) Leon Trotsky
   D) Joseph Stalin

92.
- Great degree of nationalism
- Display of military force
- Dictatorship
- Free enterprise accepted, but monitored by the state

The above issues could be used to describe which government c1930?
A) Weimar Republic of Germany
B) Fascism of Italy
C) Democracy of Great Britain
D) Communism of the Soviet Union

93. Which of the following philosophers stressed that an individual's existence is based on self-determination and free-choice?
A) Friedrich Nietzsche
B) Sigmund Freud
C) Ralph Waldo Emerson
D) Jean-Jacques Rousseau

94. Germany's annexation of Austria and remilitarization of the Rhineland during the 1930s were both examples of
A) causes of World War I
B) failures of the United Nations to keep peace
C) containment policies in Europe
D) European leaders following a policy of appeasement

95. What impact did the Invasion of Normandy (D-Day) have on the outcome of World War II?
A) The Allies opened up a second front in Europe in their fight against Germany
B) It led to a quick surrender of the Axis powers and the liberation of Berlin
C) Germany was able to rid Western Europe of an Allied presence
D) Italy was forced to surrender to the Allies in Sicily

96. Which of the following was true of the dropping of the atomic bomb in 1945?
A) The bomb only targeted weapons factories
B) Japan's citizens were never warned about the use of a new weapon
C) The action negated a need for a future military invasion of mainland Japan
D) Japan unconditionally surrendered one day after Hiroshima was bombed

97. Which of the following best describes Hitler's Final Solution?
A) Forcing Jews in Europe to wear a yellow Star of David
B) Massive deportations of Jews from Europe
C) The methodical killing of Jewish people
D) The elimination of property ownership rights and citizenship for Jews

98. What happened to Germany immediately following World War II?
A) A democratic government was allowed to unify the country
B) It was divided between World War II's Allied powers
C) The entire country fell under the control of the Soviet Union
D) The Weimar Republic was put back in power

99. I. Examples of Containment
   A. Berlin Airlift
   B. Truman Doctrine
   C. _____

Which statement would accurately represent "C" on the above outline?
A) Marshall Plan
B) Dien Bien Phu Falls
C) Russo-Japanese War
D) D-Day

100. How did Joseph Stalin's 1948 blockade of Berlin differ from the United States 1962 quarantine of Cuba?

A) Only Stalin was looking to enforce the foreign policy of containment

B) Berlin was being denied the necessities of life, while Cuba could not import weapons

C) The blockade of Berlin had the support of Britain and France

D) The Cuban blockade violated human rights treaties, while Stalin's did not

101. Which of the following is an example of détente?

A) U-2 Incident

B) Vietnam War

C) Berlin Airlift

D) SALT

102. The leadership of Mikhail Gorbachev was most associated with the

A) spreading of Roman Catholicism to Eastern Europe

B) establishment of direct democracy in the Soviet Union

C) use of brinkmanship and war against the United States

D) weakening of the Communist Party's authoritative control

103. The Korean War resulted in

A) the spreading of communism to South Korea

B) division of North and South Korea at the 17th parallel

C) massive United States aid to South Korea

D) the end of United States containment policies in Asia

104. Which of the following agendas was associated with Sun Yixian?

A) Great Leap Forward

B) Cultural Revolution

C) Three Principles

D) Four Modernizations

105. Which of the following was NOT true of the Chinese Civil War?

A) It led to the founding of the People's Republic of China

B) Japan was removed from China after World War II

C) Nationalist supporters fled to the island of Taiwan

D) The Soviet Union supported the government of Jiang Jieshi

106. Why was Mao Zedong's Great Leap Forward considered a failure?

A) Poor harvests and famine occurred

B) It led to a decrease in women's rights

C) The program temporarily removed the Communist Party from power

D) Production of materials greatly decreased

107. The Tiananmen Square massacre was a government response against protesters looking for

A) an increase in democratic reforms

B) a repeal of the Cultural Revolution

C) an end to massive industrialization

D) a way to restore the Emperor to the Chinese throne

108. Mohandas K. Gandhi's Salt March was an example of

A) demonstration by force

B) civil disobedience

C) religious insurrection

D) conformity to the British Raj

109. Why was India partitioned upon receiving independence in 1947?

A) Britain wanted to control the affairs of East Pakistan

B) Oil and other raw materials needed to be divided fairly among European nations

C) Cultural and religious differences led to the creation of new countries

D) Political divisions between Hindus led to separate national allegiances

110. What man-made structure has been important for increasing trade between the Mediterranean Sea and the Red Sea?

A) Three Gorges Dam

B) Suez Canal

C) Panama Canal

D) Aswan Dam

111. The Camp David Accords helped bring some peace to

A) Israel and Egypt

B) India and Pakistan

C) China and the United States

D) South Africa and Great Britain

112. Which of the following leaders did NOT look to embrace western ideals?

A) Nelson Mandela

B) Ayatollah Khomeini

C) Shah Mohammad Reza Pahlavi

D) Anwar Sadat

113. The roots of apartheid policies could be found in

A) tribal practices dating back centuries

B) imperialist laws set up by those of European ancestry

C) treaties established before the Boer Wars

D) negotiations accomplished at the Berlin Conference

114. Aung San Suu Kyi is associated with fighting for human rights in

A) China

B) Thailand

C) Tibet

D) Myanmar

115. The Taliban of Afghanistan supported a government based on

A) direct democracy

B) aristocracy

C) fundamentalism

D) a secular state

116. Deforestation has become an environmental issue mostly in the

A) Sahara Desert

B) Amazon Basin

C) Deccan Plateau

D) Nile River Delta

117. Nations coming together to provide tsunami relief is an example of

A) the Green Revolution

B) ethnocentrism

C) global interdependence

D) fundamentalism

118. Armenian Christians after World War I and Muslims of Bosnia-Herzegovina in the 1990s both experienced

A) human rights violations

B) westernization of Enlightenment ideas

C) religious divisions resulting from the Protestant Reformation

D) forced conversions to atheism

119. The *encomienda* system and the Middle Passage both led to

A) the expansion of the Industrial Revolution in Western Europe

B) oppression resulting from commercial endeavors

C) the spreading of Enlightenment thought throughout Eastern Europe

D) Latin American independence movements

120. The Conquistadors of the sixteenth century and the European imperialists of the nineteenth century both

A) extracted gold and diamonds from Africa

B) lost battles due to a lack of technological superiority

C) carved China into spheres of influence

D) spread Christianity around the globe

121. The Battle of Trafalgar and the defeat of the Spanish Armada were similar in that both

A) occurred in the English Channel

B) enhanced the power of the English navy

C) led to French control of overseas colonies

D) curtailed exploration in the New World

122. The Holy Alliance, Concert of Europe, and the League of Nations all looked to

A) put an end to fascist aggression in Europe

B) function as international peacekeeping organizations

C) eliminate socialist influences in the Eastern Hemisphere

D) divide African colonies among European powers

123. Robespierre's Committee of Public Information, Stalin's KGB, and Adolf Hitler's Gestapo were similar in that all

A) looked to eliminate western ideas from culture

B) attempted to silence the propaganda campaigns of the state

C) cracked down on citizens seen as acting against the national interest

D) aimed to spread communism throughout their respective nations

124. Both Peter the Great and Mustafa Kemal Atatürk

A) controlled the city of Istanbul

B) embraced Mongol culture

C) brought western ideas to their respective countries

D) favored Eastern Orthodox religious principles

125. The Five-Year Plan can best be described as

A) Vladimir Lenin's agenda to bring capitalism into a communist state

B) Mao Zedong's attempt to leap forward through collectivization

C) Joseph Stalin's plan for rapid industrialization

D) Adolf Hitler's hope to spread German living space

126. Sunni and Shi'a Muslims have historically disagreed most over

A) the degree to which westernized ideas should be introduced

B) which city should be considered the most holy

C) the proper way in which a soldier should act

D) the relationship between Muhammad and heads of state

127. How did Mao Zedong affect the lives of women?

A) He ordered the continuation of foot binding

B) He permitted women to avoid the demands of the Cultural Revolution

C) He continued the practice of women being publicly subservient

D) He offered them marriage rights

Question 128 is based on the photo below.

128. Which is true of the Hagia Sophia?

A) It was originally constructed as a mosque

B) There is evidence of Roman architecture

C) It was constructed in Western Europe

D) It was built as a monarch's palace

129. William and Mary, and Queen Victoria both supported

A) increasing the power of the absolute monarch

B) an independent Irish state

C) the increase of rights for citizens

D) expanding territory in southern Africa

130. Which statement is true of both ancient Mesopotamia and the surrounding area today?

A) A uniform legal code continues to govern the entire area

B) Geography has isolated the area from contact with other regions

C) Islam spread across the area during both time periods

D) Violence between ideologies occurs today as it did thousands of years ago

131. Religion was a contributing factor in all of the following events EXCEPT:

A) Thirty Years' War

B) Crusades

C) Sepoy Mutiny

D) The Great Purge

132. Ho Chi Minh supported

A) French control of Southeast Asia

B) the principles of communism

C) United States involvement in the Vietnam War

D) capitalist aid to South Korea

133. • Catholic Church gains immense power
• Three-Field System established
• Charlemagne becomes Holy Roman Emperor

The above events took place during which time period?

A) Middle Ages

B) Renaissance

C) Commercial Revolution

D) Ancient Greece

134. I. Major Empires of World History
  A. _____
    1. Ruled by sultans such as Suleiman the Magnificent
    2. Dominated Anatolia and the Balkans

Which Empire should be recorded into section A of the outline?
A) Mughal Empire
B) Safavid Empire
C) Ottoman Empire
D) Abbasid Empire

135. The term "developing nation" is used today to describe countries which
A) used to be communist nations
B) are the commercial leaders of the world
C) have recently adopted democratic constitutions
D) are slowly becoming industrial

# 135 Answers and Explanations

1. **B**. Algebra, calligraphy, and Islamic ceremonies held in Mecca are all related to life in the Middle East.

2. **B**. To attain enlightenment in Buddhism, one must follow the Eightfold Path, which is a moral staircase of proper behavior.

3. **D**. Islam dates back to the seventh century CE, Christianity to the first century CE, and Judaism and Hinduism date back even thousands of years earlier.

4. **A**. The Sumerians had an elaborate system of writing called *cuneiform*, which was recorded on clay tablets. The Egyptians made use of a writing system known as hieroglyphics. They used pictures and symbols to create a written record. The hieroglyphics were preserved on stone and parchment made from the papyrus plant.

5. **C**. Jerusalem was eventually taken over by Babylonian King Nebuchadnezzar II. The first Temple was destroyed, and Nebuchadnezzar put Jewish people into captivity c550 BCE.

6. **A**. Zoroastrianism is based on the teachings of Zoroaster, a prophet in Persia. The religion teaches that the forces of good and evil battle for control of the soul. It is up to a person to fend off the urges of evil. After death, one's deeds are judged. Actions on Earth determine if one is permitted to have a blissful afterlife.

7. **A**. Around 2500 BCE, there were two cities called Harappa and Mohenjo-Daro in the Indus River Valley of India. They had a complex city layout, complete with a network of roads and advanced plumbing.

8. **C**. Around 300 BCE in modern-day India, the Mauryan Empire was founded by Chandragupta. It peaked under the reign of his son, Asoka. Asoka favored Buddhism, but was tolerant of all religions.

9. **B**. India's climate is affected by great seasonal winds called *monsoons*. These impressive storms provide the rain necessary for agriculture.

10. **C**. Shi Huangdi (Qin Shi Huang) called himself the first Emperor of the Qin Dynasty. The Qin helped implement Legalism. Legalism was a belief in a strong government that kept order. It meant that the Emperor should punish those who did not carry out their civil duties. Unlike Confucianism or Daoism, Legalism meant that people had to be disciplined by the government rather than by themselves.

11. **A**. Speaker 1 reflects the Chinese philosophy of Confucianism. The Han Dynasty incorporated Confucianism into many of their daily actions including marriage and education. Those with a knowledge of Confucianism often received jobs in civil service.

12. **D**. Siddhartha Gautama, or Buddha, would speak of suffering being caused by desires. These are ideas central to Buddhism.

13. **D**. Zheng He traveled the Eastern World c1400 on fleets of ships much larger than those used by Europeans a century later.

14. **E**. The gold-salt trade was in western Africa, around the region of Ghana. Western Africa had abundant gold, but a lack of salt. Therefore, people had to travel north to trade.

15. **C**. The Mediterranean Sea led to interaction between many civilizations, including the Greeks, Romans, Egyptians, and more.

16. **C**. The Middle East is the home for Islam. The holy book of Islam is called the Qur'an.

17. **B**. Mansa Musa was a powerful king. He performed the hajj, and brought Islam to the African Empire of Mali.

18. **C**. By 10000 BCE, early humans learned that seeds could germinate into crops. The Neolithic Revolution involved just that, and the results were greater harvests, permanent settlements, and a decrease in nomadic lifestyle. Many were subsistence farmers who grew just enough to feed their families.

19. **D**. On physical maps, mountain ranges and other physical features of the Earth are noted in color or are three-dimensional.

20. **C**. The Himalayas isolated these regions from each other. The Andes are on the west coast of South America. The Urals divide Europe from Asia in Russia. The Caucasus Mountains are northeast of Turkey and southwest of Russia.

21. **B**. Terraces were like steps that went up a mountain. This allowed farming to be done on the slopes of the Andes. Rain would wash nutrients down the steps. Terrace farming was used all over the world where sloped terrain was present.

22. **B**. During the Ice Age, people traveled over a land bridge known as Beringia that connected Asia to North America (Alaska). These migrants settled and populated what would become known as the New World.

23. **B**. Teotihuacan established trade networks for the Aztecs. Tenochtitlan, near Lake Texcoco, was another major Aztec city with palaces and pyramids.

24. **A**. As big as the Mongol Empire was, they never made it to western Africa.

25. **B**. The pictured structure is the Temple of Kukulkan which can be found in the famous Mayan city of Chichen Itza.

26. **C**. The Song issued the first paper money. The Tang made block printing, which was a way to copy images. The Song later came out with movable type, where a document's letters and words could be changed at will.

27. **C**. The Gupta Empire used the concept of zero to aid in mathematical study.

28. **A**. The Mayans in the New World had an impressive knowledge of the stars and planets. In addition, the Abbasids studied the night sky during the Golden Age of Islam.

29. **D**. All three believed in a connection between the ruler on Earth to a higher religious authority.

30. **D**. Ibn Battuta traveled for 29 years all around the Eastern Hemisphere. Marco Polo was also a great traveler who visited Mongol controlled China.

31. **A**. These are statements which describe the Greek philosopher Socrates.

32. **C**. Hippocrates made great strides in medicine. Today, health care workers take a Hippocratic Oath before they practice medicine.

33. **B**. Greek city-states, such as Athens and Sparta, teamed up to defeat invaders in the Persian Wars from 490-479 BCE. The victory helped Athens usher in a new golden age of culture in the fifth century BCE.

34. **C**. An aristocracy is a term used when referring to the wealthy, or nobles. The aristocracy usually controlled much of the wealth and land of a region.

35. **C**. In Rome, patricians were the aristocracy, or rich property owners who had the most power. Plebeians were commoners such as merchants and farmers.

36. **A**. For about 100 years, there was a Mongol Peace (Pax Mongolica) that ended c1350. Much trade and cultural interaction took place during this stable time. Pax Romana was a time of about 200 years of peace in Rome from 27 BCE to 180 CE. It coincided with the rise of Augustus. This tranquil period led to greater expansion of the Roman Empire, vast trade, and cultural advances.

37. **C**. Greece and Rome paved the way for the Western culture which was experienced in Europe centuries later. This Greco-Roman culture still has a major influence on Western civilization today.

38. **B**. In 1054 there was a schism that fortified Eastern Orthodox Christianity in the Byzantine Empire. The western lands of Europe remained Roman Catholic.

39. **A**. The law prevents a citizen from being thrown into a marriage against the will of their parents.

40. **C**. At the bottom of the social order of feudalism were tax-paying peasants and serfs. Serfs were bound to the land, and could not freely travel. Serfdom existed in Russia until the nineteenth century, when Czar Alexander II emancipated (freed) them.

41. **A**. The Vikings came from the northern regions of Europe. Their dominant navy and plundering soldiers were able to secure much wealth from England during the Middle Ages.

42. **D**. Chivalry was a code of conduct where a knight fought honorably for the lord and his lady. This was similar to the Japanese bushido code of the samurai warrior.

43. **A**. During the Middle Ages, a new economic system was emerging. As part of it, many worked in business and were artisans. The merchant class was known as burghers.

44. **B.** Excommunication was a means used to kick one out of the Church. Simony was when Church positions were sold. Lay investiture was when rich nobles were appointed to be religious officials. Indulgences, or pardons from the punishments for sin, were being sold by the Church during the Middle Ages.

45. **C.** The First Crusade was called for by Pope Urban II in 1095. The purpose was to conquer the Holy Land from Muslim occupants.

46. **D.** Approximately one-third of Europe's population died from this dreaded disease. The plague was believed to be brought to Italy from Asia in 1348. It then spread to the entire continent. Italy, being a peninsula, was open to much contact and trade from other regions.

47. **B.** The Renaissance was a time period from about 1350-1550 that saw a "rebirth" of learning and culture. There was much Greco-Roman influence for this time period that came after the Dark Ages.

48. **A.** Niccolò Machiavelli wrote *The Prince* in 1513. Machiavelli believed that rulers must be strong with a ruthless personality.

49. **B.** Both of these ages of thought led to new ideas in medicine, technology, philosophy, and more. The Islamic Golden Age predated the Renaissance by centuries.

50. **C.** Renaissance paintings were secular (less concentration on religion) and done in *realism*. This meant breathtaking detailed images proportional to the human body. Renaissance art was also colorful and done in perspective, or three dimensions.

51. **D.** Henry VIII took control of the Church of England. The country eventually became Anglican, not Roman Catholic. Nearby Ireland remained Catholic.

52. **C.** Gutenberg's printing press had an enormous impact on the spreading of Martin Luther's ideas throughout Europe during the Protestant Reformation.

53. **B.** The observations would be from Central Africa. Although many practiced animism and were hunters and gatherers around the world, Bantu languages are specific to the African continent.

54. **D.** In ancient Africa, nomadic people formed clans, or small groups. Rather than living in nuclear families (with just parents and children), people typically resided with extended families (grandparents, aunts, uncles, etc.). Some families were patrilineal, meaning they traced ancestry through the father. The opposite would be matrilineal, as some societies traced it through the mother.

55. **B.** Timbuktu was a major trading center within the Songhai Empire. People traded ivory, gold, and salt.

56. **D.** Islam moved from Northern Africa through much of the Iberian Peninsula. However, Islamic Empires never took over France. Charles Martel's victory in the Battle of Tours pushed back an invasion in 732.

57. **B.** Probably the most important term of global studies, cultural diffusion means the exchange of ideas between cultures. This happened in Mesopotamia, and everywhere else in the world. Religion, technology, ideas, literature, government...you name it, it's been exchanged. As explained earlier, the Columbian Exchange transferred plants and animals between the Hemispheres as the New World was being explored. As a result of the contact, many diseases were brought as well.

58. **C.** Though looking to imitate the west, Peter's forward looking ideas predated many of Voltaire's. However, Voltaire did write a biography on him. Catherine the Great exchanged many letters with Voltaire during her reign.

59. **A.** The Edict of Milan provided tolerance towards Christians in the Roman Empire, while the Edict of Nantes gave freedoms for French Protestants, or Huguenots.

60. **D.** These acts, though years apart, limited the power of the monarch in England. As the monarch lost power, the legislating Parliament became stronger.

61. **C.** The Hapsburgs created an Empire in Central Europe, notably Austria and Hungary. After the Thirty Years' War their Empire expanded, as they conquered lands once controlled by the Ottoman Empire in the Balkans of Eastern Europe. Maria Theresa is the most relevant name to know. A devout Catholic, she was not tolerant of other religions.

62. **B.** Don't get your Roman Numerals confused! Louis (Bourbon) XIV was the prototypical absolute ruler c1700. Louis XVI was the king dethroned in the French Revolution.

63. **C.** Frederick the Great of Prussia embraced the arts, education, religious toleration, and an end to certain torture punishments.

64. **C.** Socrates, who questioned the world around him, was forced to stop teaching and was sentenced to death. Galileo's findings upset the Church, and at trial he was forced to retract his observations. Despite his retraction, Galileo spent his remaining days under house arrest.

65. **B.** Gandhi protested laws he saw as unjust (civil disobedience), while Rousseau believed that "chains," or unjust laws, should be resisted.

66. **A.** In 1792, the British activist Mary Wollstonecraft published *A Vindication of the Rights of Woman*. She argued that women should receive an equal education to men, and participate in politics and the economy outside of the home. Still, it would be decades before women received equality in Europe.

67. **B.** A branch of the Third Estate was the bourgeoisie. They were well-educated artisans and capitalists who familiarized themselves with Enlightenment thought. The bourgeoisie believed they were entitled to a say in government because of their education and standing in society.

68. **B.** In the aftermath of the Reign of Terror, the moderate Directory took power. They appointed Napoleon Bonaparte to lead France's army. He suddenly seized power in 1799. Such a "blow of state" is called a *coup d'état*.

69. **B.** Geography played a part in their failures to conquer Britain and Russia. Britain, an island, possessed a strong navy and is protected by water. Russia is enormous and has harsh winters.

70. **C.** The Declaration was a vital document for the French Revolution and inspired independence movements in Latin America. Remember: The American Revolution came before the French uprising, and therefore choice B isn't correct.

71. **D.** Haiti was the scene of a slave uprising against the French which was led at first by Toussaint L'Ouverture. Most Latin American independence movements were against Spain. Brazil gained independence from Portugal.

72. **D.** Both unification movements relied strongly on nationalistic sentiment, as people had pride in their nation because of a common culture, history, language, and set of beliefs.

73. **C.** This is an excerpt from Rudyard Kipling's *The White Man's Burden*, which addressed the subject of imperialism.

74. **D.** Bismarck unified Germany with "Blood and Iron," as through war, Prussia won land.

75. **A.** Speaker 2 is Charles Darwin. Darwin's theory of evolution was very controversial, as it did not conform to the teachings of the Bible.

76. **B.** Speaker 4 is Adam Smith, author of the *The Wealth of Nations*. He supported a free market, competition, and *laissez-faire*, where the government would keep its "hands off" the economy.

77. **A.** *The Communist Manifesto* is concerned with the divisions of classes which resulted from the rapid changes of the Industrial Revolution.

78. **A.** Japan never turned to communism in the twentieth century. The other countries were affected by communism.

79. **B.** Urbanization means the migration of people from rural areas to cities. With transportation improving, much urbanization took place during the Industrial Revolution.

80. **A.** Captain Alfred Dreyfus was a Jewish military officer who was accused of selling secrets to the Germans. He was found guilty after fellow officers set him up for conviction. The pogroms were persecutions against Jews living in Russia under Czar Alexander III.

81. **B.** All of these events looked to expel foreign imperialists, most notably Great Britain. These events happened in the nineteenth century, well after the French Revolution had ended.

82. **D.** Europeans looked to imperialize in the nineteenth century to increase riches and gain markets for the products of the Empire. Along the way, religion and culture were spread to foreign lands.

83. **A.** The spark that started the war was the assassination which took place in Sarajevo on June 28, 1914. It occurred when Archduke Franz Ferdinand was shot by Serbian nationalist Gavrilo Princip.

84. **C.** Britain gained control of Hong Kong with the Treaty of Nanjing. Be careful…if you chose choice D, you are a bit too far north.

85. **A**. After World War I, Japan invaded northern China in Manchuria. They used the territory to increase their raw material resources before World War II.

86. **B**. The Ottoman Empire was quickly losing both power and land. Its nickname at the onset of World War I was the "sick man" of Europe in the "powder keg" of the Balkans.

87. **B**. Months after American reinforcements arrived, Kaiser Wilhelm II agreed to an armistice (ceasefire) to end the fighting on November 11, 1918. This happened in the eleventh hour of the eleventh day of the eleventh month.

88. **A**. Wilson's fourteenth point in his speech would eventually become the League of Nations. However, President Wilson's United States would neither ratify the Treaty of Versailles or join the League.

89. **B**. After dropping out of the war, Russia lost Estonia, Ukraine, Finland, Latvia, and Lithuania.

90. **C**. The Czar was brought down partially because of the other three choices. Choice C occurred after the Czar was overthrown when the communists took over Russia.

91. **B**. Before the Bolsheviks came to power months later, there was a Provisional Government which ultimately was directed by Alexander Kerensky.

92. **B**. Fascism is a political ideology where a dictator promotes nationalism under the threat of extensive military force. In Italy, Mussolini displayed military force, opposed communism, and despite the appearance of free enterprise, controlled much of the economy.

93. **A**. The Nazis relied on the century-old philosophy of German Friedrich Nietzsche. They selectively quoted him to criticize democracy. Nietzsche was an *existentialist*, meaning he stressed that an individual's existence is based on self-determination and free-choice.

94. **D**. Because the League of Nations had no army to stop him, Hitler disobeyed the Treaty of Versailles and increased the size of his army. Europe did not stand in his way, and thereby *appeased* him, or gave into the aggressor with hopes of avoiding war.

95. **A**. The Allies invaded northern France on 6/6/1944. After penetrating into Nazi occupied areas, they were able to fortify a second front against Germany. Russia was already fighting from the east, and now the rest of the Allies were attacking Germany from the west.

96. **C**. President Truman decided a mainland invasion of Japan would be too costly in terms of casualties, so he put in the order for the *Enola Gay* to drop *Little Boy* (the Atomic Bomb). On August 6, 1945 Hiroshima was bombed resulting in the deaths of about 140,000 people. Nagasaki was bombed three days later leading to an estimated 70,000 deaths.

97. **C**. As the war progressed, the elimination of Jews became a priority for the Nazis. The Final Solution was genocide, or the methodical killing of European Jews. Before the Final Solution, Jews lost their rights with the Nuremberg Laws, and were later forced to live in reserved areas called ghettos.

98. **B**. After the war, Germany was divided into occupational zones controlled by the Soviet Union in the East, and Allies (Britain, France, and the United States) in the West.

99. **A.** The economic aid given out by the Marshall Plan is an example of containment, or stopping the spread of communism.

100. **B.** Soviet leader Joseph Stalin, wanting to keep Germany divided, blockaded the highway and rail resources coming into West Berlin (the non-communist side). This prevented food and other necessities from reaching the people. The Cuban blockade aimed to prevent missiles or other Soviet weaponry from reaching Cuba during the Cuban Missile Crisis.

101. **D.** Détente means the easing of Cold War tensions. SALT, or the Strategic Arms Limitation Talks, resulted in a 1972 treaty which looked to limit nuclear weapons in superpower arsenals.

102. **D.** With Mikhail Gorbachev's rule over the Soviet Union there was a new outlook. The policies of glasnost (openness) and perestroika (economic restructuring) weakened the authoritative communist state.

103. **C.** The Korean War ended in 1953 leaving an estimated death toll in the millions. In the aftermath, massive American aid poured into South Korea for decades. The 38th parallel is still the dividing line in Korea today, as North and South Korea are buffered by a demilitarized zone (DMZ).

104. **C.** Sun Yixian offered Three Principles to the Chinese people (People's Rule/Nationalism, Democracy, and People's Livelihood). His leadership helped dethrone the Qing Dynasty. The Great Leap Forward and Cultural Revolution were Mao Zedong's agendas, while the Four Modernizations program was expanded by Deng Xiaoping.

105. **D.** Jieshi would be supported by the United States who was looking to stop the spread of Mao Zedong's communist forces.

106. **A.** Despite the increase in production, the Great Leap Forward was mostly a failure because bad weather and depleted agricultural workforces led to poor harvests and famines that killed millions. Furthermore, there was an overproduction of shoddy finished goods.

107. **A.** In 1989, students protested communist rule and peacefully campaigned for democracy in Beijing's Tiananmen Square. Deng Xiaoping's soldiers opened fire, killing many protesters.

108. **B.** Gandhi practiced civil disobedience, or disobeying laws seen as unjust. The Indian people were forced to purchase salt from the British Raj (name for British rule). This salt was taxed. Gandhi and his followers protested this British monopoly by marching 240 miles to the coastal city of Dandi to get their own salt. As the movement for salt escalated, British authorities violently beat the protesters.

109. **C.** Cultural and religious differences fostered the need for partitioning. India was mostly Hindu, while Islam influenced Pakistan.

110. **B.** The Suez Canal was completed in 1869, and controlled by European nations as a means to connect the Red Sea to the Mediterranean Sea. Egypt's leader, Gamal Abdel Nasser, took control of the canal in 1956.

111. **A.** This was one of the rare peace agreements in the Middle East. Menachem Begin of Israel, Anwar Sadat of Egypt, and President Jimmy Carter of the United States met at Camp David in Maryland. There, it was agreed that Egypt would recognize Israel as a nation-state, and Israel would give back the Sinai Peninsula.

112. **B.** Ayatollah Khomeini supported an Islamic state in Iran, not a westernized one. He helped lead the Iranian Revolution in 1979.

113. **B.** Given self-rule from Great Britain, the Republic of South Africa's white National Party members and Afrikaners (Dutch descendants) discriminated against black Africans in a policy known as apartheid.

114. **D.** In Myanmar (formerly called Burma), the military ruled through dictatorship. Aung San Suu Kyi was instrumental in a nonviolent protest movement for democracy and human rights. Despite winning the 1991 Nobel Peace Prize, she spent over a decade as a political prisoner. After being freed in 2010, she won a parliament seat in 2012.

115. **C.** The Taliban controlled a *fundamentalist* (strict adherence to religious principles) Islamic government in Afghanistan c2000. They isolated themselves from most of the Western World.

116. **B.** The Amazon River is surrounded by millions of trees. Many trees have become subject to logging, or have been cleared away for human dwellings.

117. **C.** In recent years, nations have become dependent on each other. They also can have their livelihood affected by events thousands of miles away. This sense of oneness is considered part of global interdependence.

118. **A.** When the Ottoman Empire collapsed, Armenian Christians faced persecutions, deportation, famine, and were the targets of violence. In Bosnia-Herzegovina, ethnic cleansing, or the violent elimination of a group from an area, occurred as Serbian forces attempted to remove Muslim influences from Bosnia.

119. **B.** With new capitalistic endeavors in the Western Hemisphere (New World), there was a demand for labor in the sixteenth century. The Middle Passage was the central journey and slave trade of the Triangular Trade. *Encomienda* was a Spanish system of forced labor against Native Americans.

120. **D.** The Spanish brought Christianity to the New World in the sixteenth century. In the nineteenth century, European powers brought Christianity all around the world, most notably to Africa and Asia.

121. **B.** In 1588, England defeated the Spanish Armada. They defeated Napoleon at the Battle of Trafalgar in 1805. Both events legitimized their navy.

122. **B.** Fearful of revolutions similar to the one seen in France, coalitions such as the Holy Alliance and Metternich's Concert of Europe were formed. The League of Nations was created after World War I also to promote peace.

123. **C.** All three were police organizations that looked to crush citizens who were viewed as traitors.

124. **C.** Both Peter the Great and Mustafa Kemal Atatürk modernized their nations with Western ideas. Peter did so in Russia while Atatürk westernized the Republic of Turkey.

125. **C.** Stalin made a series of Five-Year Plans which aimed to modernize industry in the Soviet Union. The plan looked to produce raw materials such as coal and iron, and extend railway lines, electricity, and communication networks.

126. **D.** A caliph is a religious leader who is also the head of the government. The Shi'a Muslims believe that the caliph should be a relative of Muhammad. The Sunnis disagree and state that rulers could lead as long as they preach his ideas. Still today, these two groups experience violent conflict.

127. **D.** Mao offered an increase in women's rights. This meant marriage rights and an end to being publicly subservient. After he secured power, women were expected to provide for the state as well as their families.

128. **B.** Emperor Justinian supported a unification of church and state. His most ornate church, the Hagia Sophia, eventually became a mosque when the Ottoman Empire conquered Constantinople (now called Istanbul). The Byzantines preserved Roman architecture, building structures with domes and arches.

129. **C.** Though centuries apart, these monarchs looked to increase the rights of the people. William and Mary took over England after the Glorious Revolution. They adopted the Bill of Rights. Queen Victoria was known for spreading democracy to the people. During her reign, there was a working class Chartist Movement which demanded more rights, such as suffrage (voting privileges) for men.

130. **D.** Ancient Mesopotamia saw the cultural clashes of warring groups such as Babylonians, Sumerians, and Akkadians. The Fertile Crescent can be found in modern-day Iraq, an area which has been hampered by warring conflict.

131. **D.** Joseph Stalin's Great Purge targeted government officials in the Communist Party and peasants who were seen as enemies of the state.

132. **B.** In 1954, the French saw the city of Dien Bien Phu fall to the communists and their leader Ho Chi Minh. Minh used nationalism as a unifying force to drive out the French, and spread communism.

133. **A.** All of these events took place during the Middle Ages. The Middle Ages are what historians call the time period in Europe between roughly 500-1500. This was an era when Europe slowly evolved after the Fall of Rome.

134. **C.** Suleiman the Magnificent was a sultan in the Ottoman Empire. The Empire was named for Osman I. At its peak, the Ottoman Empire dominated Anatolia, the Balkans, and Northern Africa.

135. **D.** Developing nations are those who are becoming industrialized. Developed nations have established themselves as having manufacturing centers and more advanced economies.

# Notes: